Nature Guide to SOUTH EAST ENGLAND

Hampshire, Kent, Surrey, Sussex & the Isle of Wight

JOHN SANKEY

Contents

Cover photographs:
Top: Hobby, Round-headed Rampion,
Marsh Grasshopper on Bog Myrtle
Centre: Bee Orchid, Roe Deer, Chalkhill
Blue
Bottom: Beech Woods at High Wray
Title page photograph *(page 1)*:
Oast houses, Kent

**Edited by Helen Gilks
and Su Swallow**

Series Editor: Karen Goaman

Designed by Anne Sharples

The editor wishes to thank Casey Horton and
Pauline Khng for help in the editorial production of
this book, and Mary Fane for picture research.

The author and publishers wish to thank the
following people and organizations for their help:
Dr June Chatfield of the Wakes Museum
Selborne, County Councils of Kent, Surrey, East
and West Sussex, Hampshire, and Medina
Borough Council (Isle of Wight). Hampshire and
Isle of Wight Naturalists' Trust, Hampshire Field
Club, Hampshire Ornithological Society, Mr A
Holcombe of Ornitholidays, Kent Field Club, Kent
Ornithological Society, Kent, Surrey and Sussex
Trusts for Nature Conservation, Miss C
Lipscombe, National Farmers Union, National
Federation of Young Farmers Clubs, National
Trust, Nature Conservancy Council, Royal
Society for the Protection of Birds, Surrey Bird
Club, Sussex Ornithological Society.

The author also wishes to thank his publishers
whose staff have at all times provided friendly and
helpful advice without which this book would
never have appeared.

Most of the illustrations in the section on pages
33–96, Common Species of the Countryside and
Seashore, have been previously published in the
Usborne Spotter's Guides series.

First published in 1981 by
Usborne Publishing Limited
20 Garrick Street, London WC2

Printed and bound in Great Britain by
Fakenham Press Limited, Fakenham, Norfol

Introduction

Despite its density of population, the South-East offers a great diversity of landscapes and wildlife habitats. Along the coast, imposing chalk cliffs contrast with the lonely mudflats and dyke-bordered fields of Romney Marsh and the Isle of Sheppey. Inland, there are rolling Downs, with a fascinating range of plants flourishing on their chalky soils, Beechwoods, Oak forests, conifer plantations and heathland tinged purple with Ling. High hedgebanks border country lanes and riverbanks are lined with flowers. Each habitat supports a particular range of wildlife and flourishes amidst hop gardens, orchards, downland farms, ancient Saxon-patterned villages and modern towns.

A number of nature trails, museums, superb view points, beautiful gardens and houses can be enjoyed in the region and contribute to a better understanding of the precious heritage in the landscape and wildlife of Kent, Surrey, Sussex, Hampshire and the Isle of Wight. No country lover can fail to find something of interest, be it by freshwater, along the coast or on chalk, sand or clay soils.

▲ Typical Downs landscape in Hampshire – grassy slopes, with an isolated clump of trees, giving way to cultivated fields.

How to use this Book

The first section of this book, pages 4-32, illustrated with colour photographs and paintings, describes the habitats that are characteristic of the South-East and the animals and plants special to the region. There are colour maps on pages 4-7 showing the main areas in which the habitats described occur. Many habitats are closely linked to the geology and climatic conditions of the region, and these features are also described, on pages 8-9.

The middle section of the book, pages 33-96, contains illustrations of over 350 species of animals and plants commonly found in the South-East and over much of Britain. Further details on how to use this section are found on page 33.

The third section of the book, "Places to Visit", found on pages 97-121, consists of a gazetteer containing descriptions of over 200 places of interest. Each county has a separate list and a map showing the location of the sites. The places described include specific habitats, nature reserves, nature trails, birdwatching points, and also zoos, wildlife parks, country parks, gardens and museums. Further details on how to use this section are found on page 97.

Information such as useful addresses, good reference books and a full index are found at the end of the book. Use the index to find out whether a species is illustrated — page numbers referring to illustrations appear in bold.

When visiting the countryside, care should be taken to respect the habitats and the wildlife living there. Flowers should not be picked, nesting birds and mammals with young should not be disturbed, and the Country Code, set out on page 122, should always be followed. Some of the problems related to nature conservation are also discussed on page 122.

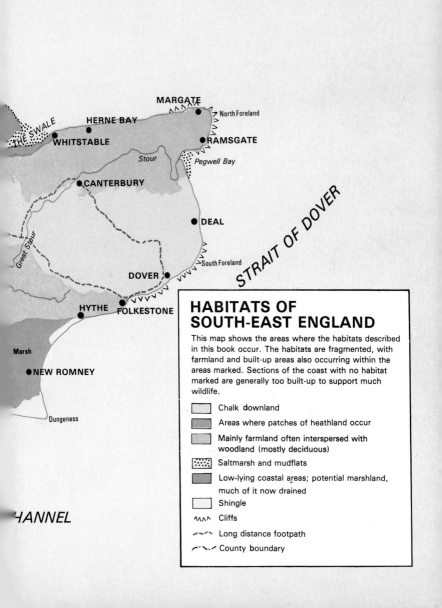

MARGATE

THE SWALE

HERNE BAY

WHITSTABLE

North Foreland

RAMSGATE

Stour

Pegwell Bay

CANTERBURY

Great Stour

DEAL

STRAIT OF DOVER

South Foreland

DOVER

HYTHE
FOLKESTONE

Marsh

NEW ROMNEY

Dungeness

CHANNEL

HABITATS OF SOUTH-EAST ENGLAND

This map shows the areas where the habitats described in this book occur. The habitats are fragmented, with farmland and built-up areas also occurring within the areas marked. Sections of the coast with no habitat marked are generally too built-up to support much wildlife.

Chalk downland

Areas where patches of heathland occur

Mainly farmland often interspersed with woodland (mostly deciduous)

Saltmarsh and mudflats

Low-lying coastal areas; potential marshland, much of it now drained

Shingle

ᴧᴧᴧ Cliffs

⌒⌒⌒ Long distance footpath

⌒·⌒ County boundary

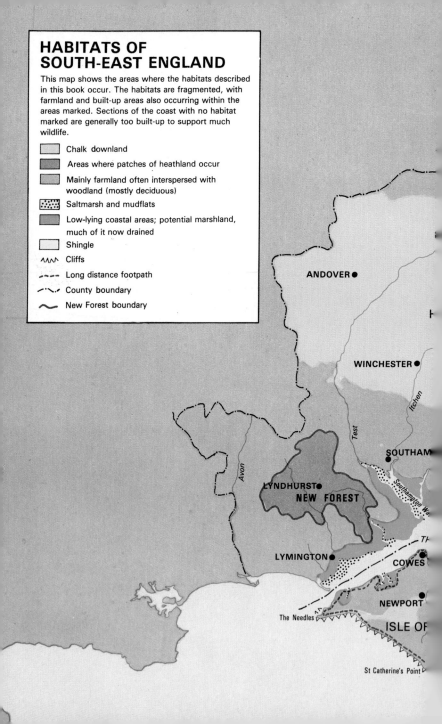

HABITATS OF SOUTH-EAST ENGLAND

This map shows the areas where the habitats described in this book occur. The habitats are fragmented, with farmland and built-up areas also occurring within the areas marked. Sections of the coast with no habitat marked are generally too built-up to support much wildlife.

- Chalk downland
- Areas where patches of heathland occur
- Mainly farmland often interspersed with woodland (mostly deciduous)
- Saltmarsh and mudflats
- Low-lying coastal areas; potential marshland, much of it now drained
- Shingle
- ʌʌʌ Cliffs
- ---- Long distance footpath
- ⌐·ˍ· County boundary
- ⌐ New Forest boundary

ANDOVER●

WINCHESTER●

SOUTHAM

Test

Itchen

LYNDHURST●
NEW FOREST

Avon

LYMINGTON●

Southampton Wa

Th

COWES●

NEWPORT●

The Needles ʌʌʌʌ

St Catherine's Point

ISLE OF

Geology and Climate

Rocks and Soils

The varied landscape of the South-East provides a wide variety of wildlife habitats, ranging from saltmarshes and cliffs along the coast to grassland, farmland, woods and heaths inland. Each habitat is clearly distinguished by its vegetation. The change from one kind of vegetation to another, which may be quite sudden, is closely related to the type of rock and also to the soil, on which plants grow.

There are three main types of rock in the area: chalk, sandstone and clay. One of the main geological features of the South-East is a sweeping band of chalk which runs from Salisbury Plain into Hampshire where it splits to form the North Downs of Surrey and Kent, and the South Downs of Sussex. Chalk soils are typically thin and porous and were it not for a thin band of clay, called Gault, which runs underneath the Downs and prevents water from completely draining through the Chalk, the Downs would be a virtual desert. Gault forms a thin band at the edge of the Downs where it reaches the surface. In places on the Downs, deposits of clay, sands, flints and gravels overlie the chalk, giving rise to deeper, damper soils where woodland can develop. Where the chalk Downs meet the coast, spectacular white cliffs may occur, as around Dover and Beachy Head.

In between the North and South Downs, and including their scarp slopes, lies a region of scarps and vales, known as the Weald. The Weald can be divided into a number of natural regions which are closely related to the underlying rocks. The High Weald lies predominantly on sandy soil, with deposits of clay in the valleys. This area contains some fertile soils and it is here that the fruit orchards and hop farms of Kent are situated. In other places, as in the Ashdown Forest, the soil tends to be acid and deficient in minerals. These soils are rarely cultivated and either support heathland vegetation or may be planted with conifers.

Surrounding the High Weald is the Low Weald, a generally low-lying area where clay predominates. Although very fertile the soil is somewhat intractable, even to modern agricultural machinery, and as a

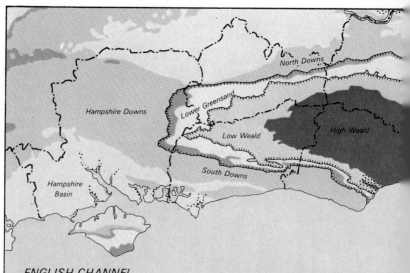

ENGLISH CHANNEL

**ROCKS AND SOILS
OF SOUTH-EAST ENGLAND**

result, areas of cultivated land are still interspersed with woodland and pastures.

Between the Low Weald and the Downs lies an area of sandstone known as the Lower Greensand. Like the High Weald, this area contains some fertile farmland, more especially in Kent, and some areas of heathland, mainly in Surrey and Sussex.

Between the North Downs and the Thames Estuary is a highly cultivated slope composed partly of chalky soils and, on the lower lying areas, of clays, sands and gravels. Where this slope meets the sea it is often overlaid with deposits of alluvium which give rise to marshland and saltmarshes. Similarly where the clay soils of the Weald meet the south coast, deposits of alluvium also occur. This alluvium once supported extensive marshlands, as at Romney Marsh and Pevensey Levels, but today much of this has been drained to provide valuable farmland.

To the south of the Hampshire Downs lies the Hampshire Basin, an area largely composed of sands and gravels with some clay, which give rise to the mixed habitats of heath and woodland of the New Forest.

The Isle of Wight, while physically separate, is virtually an outdoor geological museum, containing within its area most of the rocks found in the rest of the region.

Climate

The South-East has a relatively mild and dry climate, rarely subject to sudden extremes. With prevailing weather coming from the west, rain and winds tend to disperse and die out before reaching the eastern regions of England. Naturally there is some regional variation, and coastal areas, especially those directly facing the English Channel, receive the full force of westerly gales. Along the east Kent coast and the Thames Estuary easterly winds become more evident and in general this area is cooler than elsewhere in the region. Mean January temperatures range from 5.6°C to 4.4°C from west to east, and in July from 16.7°C to 17.2°C again from west to east.

Most of the region has an annual rainfall of between 620 and 750 mm; slightly more falls on the higher parts of the Downs and slightly less on low-lying coastal areas.

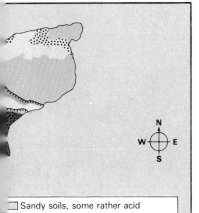

Sandy soils, some rather acid
Sandy soils with clay in valleys
Sands and gravels with some clay
Gault
Weald clay
Chalk
Alluvium
County boundaries
Scarp slopes

▲ An old quarry on the Downs showing the whiteness of the chalk and the thin soil which typically overlies this type of rock.

▼ View from Box Hill on the North Downs with the grassy turf of the chalk giving way to the heavily wooded clay soils of the Low Weald.

Downland

The Downs of the South-East are characterized by gently sloping hills covered with springy turf. These open grasslands are grazed by sheep and are interspersed with patches of scrub, woodland and farmland.

The soil of the Downs is predominantly chalky but in much of the North Downs and parts of West Sussex and the Hampshire Downs, the chalk is overlayed with deposits of clay and flint (Clay-with-Flints) or other rocks, which usually give rise to a deeper, more fertile soil. These areas are often quite heavily wooded and Oak trees in particular, which rarely grow on thin chalky soil, are usually present.

Elsewhere on the Downs, especially in Hampshire and West Sussex, small clumps of trees, or "caps" stand out clearly in the open scenery. These may be growing on isolated deposits of Clay-with-Flints or other rocks. "Hangers" are another feature of the Downs. These are areas of Beech woodland at the top of steep-sided valleys and escarpments.

Caps and hangers have usually been planted. Trees commonly found on the Downs, but by no means confined to chalky soils, include Ash, Beech and Yew.

Areas of open grassland are an attractive feature of the Downs. Sheep have grazed on the South Downs for more than 2000 years and more recently rabbits and cattle have joined the sheep in preventing the growth of scrub and woodland that would otherwise develop naturally. Although chalk soil is deficient in some minerals, it supports an exciting variety of plant species, including many which only grow on chalk rich soils. From spring to autumn there are always some plants in flower on the Downs and many can be identified at all times of the year by their vegetative character.

Apart from those shown on these pages, other plants typical of chalky soils include the Bulbous Buttercup, Common Rockrose, Rough Hawkbit, Ploughman's Spikenard, Small Scabious, Common Milkwort and Salad Burnet.

▼ A characteristic South Downs scene with open farmland and grazing sheep. Chanctonbury Ring, a clump of Beech trees, caps the higher ground and is a well-known landmark.

▲ A number of beautiful orchid species grow on the Downs; they may be common one year and scarce the next. The scented Fragrant Orchid (*left*) sometimes grows in large numbers, often with the Common Spotted Orchid (*centre*). The Bee Orchid (*right*) may have up to seven flowers on its tall stem.

▼ Marjoram (*left*) grows in rough grassland; its leaves, when crushed, smell of mint and are used as a cooking herb. The Carline Thistle (*centre*) grows in grassland on all parts of the Downs while Round-headed Rampion (*right*) is mainly confined to rough Downs pastures of Sussex.

▼ Autumn Gentian (*left*), Yellow-wort (*centre*) and Clustered Bellflower (*right*) flower on the Downs grassland until late September. The leaves of Yellow-wort grow in pairs, joined at their base around the stem; Clustered Bellflower sometimes occurs with white flowers.

Other plants common on the Downs but not confined to chalky soils include Harebell, Viper's Bugloss, White Bryony, Wild Strawberry and, especially on ant hills, Wild Thyme. Deadly Nightshade, a bush with very poisonous blue-black berries, is usually found in old chalk quarries or on disturbed chalky soils.

Many orchids grow on the Downs and a number of species, such as the Musk, Lady and Man Orchids, are only to be found on chalk soils of the South-East.

On areas that are not heavily grazed, scrub tends to develop. Apart from those illustrated on page 13, the plants that commonly form scrub are Buckthorn, Bramble, Dog Rose, Dogwood, Hawthorn, Sweet Briar and Wild Privet. Old Man's Beard, always an indicator of chalk soil, is often seen growing over these shrubs. Many birds are attracted to areas of scrub; some, like finches and thrushes, for the berries that many of the bushes bear in autumn, and others, such as warblers, for the rich variety of insect life that scrub supports. Scrub also provides suitable nesting sites for many birds.

▲ The rare Lady Orchid is now confined to wooded areas on the Downs in Kent. It flowers in May and June, and has several large shiny leaves.

▼ Sainfoin may be seen in grassland on the Downs from June to September; it is sometimes cultivated as a fodder crop.

▼ Stemless Thistle grows in a rosette close to the ground and is often found in the short turf of the Downs.

▼ Kidney Vetch is an important food plant for some of the Blue Butterfly caterpillars. A red flowering variety also occurs, usually by the sea.

▼ Hairy Violet is one of the first plants of the year to flower on the Downs (in April); occasionally a white-flowered variety occurs.

Despite the extent of cultivated land and grazed grassland, there is an abundance of animal life. The Downs offer a wide variety of habitats where birds can nest and feed; many species can be seen all the year round, while others are summer or winter visitors. Among the common migrants are the Redwing and Fieldfare, two species of thrush that migrate to Britain in the autumn from their breeding grounds in northern Europe. These birds often flock together on farmland, scrub, woods or open grassland, where they feed on wild fruits, grains and small animals, such as earthworms, snails and beetles.

Finches also gather in flocks in winter; groups of Bramblings and Chaffinches, for example, may be seen on open ground feeding on seeds, or under Beech trees where they feed on Beech mast (nuts). In spring, Bramblings may be seen preparing to return to their breeding grounds in Scandinavia and Siberia. The Wheatear is a summer visitor to Britain and may be seen on the Downs bobbing along the ground as it hunts for insects.

▼ Many plants that form scrub bear colourful berries in the autumn. Whitebeam, Wayfaring Tree and Elder have clusters of white flowers in early summer. Old Man's Beard and Spindle have small, inconspicuous greenish-yellow flowers.

Whitebeam

Wayfaring Tree

Spindle

Old Man's Beard

Elder

Several birds that breed in rough open country find suitable nesting sites on the Downs. The Meadow Pipit and Corn Bunting build their grassy nests on or near the ground while the Lapwing lays its eggs in a scrape, usually on open ploughed ground. The Corn Bunting has no distinctive markings but can often be seen on its song post – anything from a clod of earth to a high branch. It has a high-pitched, jangling song.

One of the most typical sounds on a summer day on the South Downs is the melodious song of the Skylark. Flushed from its feeding spot on the ground it soars almost vertically, then hovers in the sky, singing all the time. Though quite rare, Buzzards can occasionally be seen soaring over open downland near woods.

Rabbits and Brown Hares live on the open grasslands and Foxes and Badgers may be seen in the evening when they emerge from the woodlands to feed. Roe Deer inhabit the more wooded areas of the North Downs.

Much of the animal life of the Downs consists of smaller creatures like snails, spiders, grasshoppers, bees, butterflies and moths. Unlike many plants, few of these animals are specifically confined to chalkland although snails, which need the calcium contained in chalk to form their shells, are particularly numerous on the Downs.

Small grassy mounds reveal the presence of the Yellow Meadow Ant. These ant hills should not be confused with mole hills, which are piles of freshly thrown up soil that collapse before turf has spread over them.

Some of the typical butterflies of open downland are those that lay their eggs on common chalkland plants which provide food for the caterpillars. The caterpillars of the Chalkhill Blue, the Adonis Blue and the Common Blue feed on Horseshoe Vetch; the Common Blue also feeds on Kidney Vetch, Bird's Foot Trefoil, Clovers and Black Medick which are all typical chalkland plants.

Several members of the Skipper family, named after their darting flight, are common. The Grizzled Skipper caterpillar feeds on the leaves of Wild Strawberry and other plants, and that of the Dingy Skipper on Bird's Foot Trefoil and Horseshoe Vetch. The Marbled White, with its chessboard-like markings, may be seen especially on thistle flowers.

▲ The Brambling has a distinct white rump. The male (not shown) has a dark brown head.

▼ The Goldfinch frequents hedges and scrub on the Downs; it often feeds on thistle seeds.

▼ The Red-legged Partridge may be seen in grassland and along hedgerows of the Downs.

▲ The Lapwing – also called Peewit after its call – nests on open ploughed downland and may be seen in large flocks in winter.

▲ The Cuckoo often lays its egg in the nest of the Meadow Pipit. After hatching, the young Cuckoo ejects its host's young from the nest.

▲ The Redwing can be seen on the Downs in winter; it has a light line through its eye and reddish flanks, visible when in flight.

▲ Britain's largest snail, the Roman Snail, occurs locally on the North Downs. In recent years its numbers have declined.

▲ The Silver-spotted Skipper is not common but may be seen in grassland on the Downs.

▲ The day-flying Six-spot Burnet Moth is a common sight all over the Downs.

▼ The Downs are one of the few areas where the beautiful Adonis Blue may be seen in England.

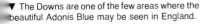

▼ The Chalkhill Blue, the largest of the Blues, occurs locally in colonies on chalk areas.

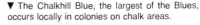

Rivers

The rivers of the South-East provide some of the most delightful scenery of the area and are also particularly rich in wildlife. This is partly because they are comparatively unpolluted, undisturbed and their waters less acid than those of many rivers in other parts of Britain. They are also in a region where the climate is slightly warmer than that of most other regions.

Along the banks of these rivers, many of which are rich in chalk, a profusion of colourful and elegant plants grow. Many riverside plants reproduce from creeping roots rather than from seed; seeds could too easily be carried away by water or fall on the landward side of the bank where it would be too dry for them to grow.

A number of plants introduced from abroad have now established themselves along the rivers. Himalayan Balsam is one example, and its beautiful pink flowers are now conspicuous on most river banks. Its pointed seed-capsules burst in the sun's heat thus scattering the seeds; the warmth of one's fingers can have the same effect – hence this plant's other name, Indian Touch-me-not. Besides those shown here, other common plants on river banks in the region are Skullcap, Great Willowherb, the poisonous Hemlock and Hemlock Water Dropwort. Plants growing in river waters include Yellow Waterlily, Water Crowfoot and Starwort.

The leaves of riverside plants are sometimes studded with the blue and red Reed Beetles, and Water Mint may harbour the brilliant green Mint Beetle. Other noticeable insects along rivers are the slow-flying Damselflies with their smoky green or blue-blotched wings.

Several birds nest in the vicinity of fresh water and may be seen along rivers, especially stretches where the current is slow-flowing. Moorhen, Coot, Mallard and Mute Swan are some of the commoner species. The Kingfisher, with its unmistakeable blue plumage is attracted to areas of river with sandy banks and a good supply of fish. The Heron, standing motionless on one leg in the shallows, is not an uncommon sight. A recent arrival, Cetti's Warbler, usually follows rivers in the South-East; its loud flute-like voice is unlike that of any other warbler.

The Water Vole and Water Shrew may sometimes be seen on river banks and the Otter, now very scarce, is still worth looking out for along the Hampshire rivers. The North American Mink has unfortunately become wild in places along some of the rivers, having escaped from captivity. The Mink is a voracious eater, feeding on fish, crayfish, voles, birds and almost any kind of meat available. Like the introduced Grey Squirrel, it does considerable damage to our native wildlife.

▼ A stretch of the River Itchen with patches of Water Crowfoot growing in its waters.

▼ The Kingfisher dives headlong from flight, or from a perch, to catch fish.

▲ The Mink inhabits wooded stretches of rivers and streams. It is a powerful swimmer and is often mistaken for the much larger Otter.

▲ The Monkey Flower, introduced from N. America, has now established itself along river banks where it often grows in large clumps.

▲ Branched Bur-reed (*left*) is a common plant of river banks; it bears inconspicuous greenish flowers which develop into burs. Yellow Loosestrife (*centre*), its leaves often dotted with black spots, and the unrelated Purple Loosestrife (*right*) make colourful displays along rivers from June to August.

▼ Common Reeds (*left*) grow by water, fresh or salty, and provide cover and nesting sites for a number of birds. Hemp Agrimony (*centre*) is a tall plant with clusters of pink flowers that attract butterflies. The flowers of the Yellow Iris (*right*) may be seen by rivers from June to August.

Woodland

Two thousand years ago large areas of Britain were covered with forest but today only fragments of these remain. Parts of the Weald – an area once covered with a vast tract of forest – and of the New Forest are still quite heavily wooded, but elsewhere in the South-East, woodland occurs only in more scattered patches.

Most types of vegetation, if undisturbed by man, will naturally be replaced by woodland. Grassland, for example, if not subjected to ploughing, grazing, cutting or burning, will in time be invaded by bushes and then by trees. This process is called plant succession and woods represent the end phase or climax of this succession.

The type of woodland that occurs varies according to the type of soil. Generally, the lighter chalky soils support Beech while heavier clay soils support Oak. On lighter, less fertile, sandy soils, Scots Pine is often the dominant tree, with Sessile Oak growing where the sandy soil is less impoverished. Plantations of non-native evergreens for timber production are also found mainly on sandy soils. Corsican Pine, European Larch, Spruce and Western Hemlock are trees typical of these plantations.

Coppicing, as a means of timber production, is still a feature of some of the woodlands. Sweet Chestnut and sometimes Hazel or, more rarely Hornbeam, are periodically cut down to the base; the new shoots that grow up from the cut stump provide wood suitable for poles, broom handles, fencing and other uses. Old coppiced trees, if left uncut, have several trunks instead of one.

Nearly all woods have several easily-distinguished layers: the tree canopy, the shrub layer, the field layer of non-woody plants, and the moss and leaf litter layer. Quite a number of plants of the shrub and field layers have special means of obtaining as much light as possible. Plants like Honeysuckle climb towards light using trees and bushes as support; many plants flower and produce seeds early in the year before the trees have come into full leaf.

▼ Beechwoods are very much a feature of the South-East, being the dominant type of woodland on chalk soils. In autumn, the trees bear fruit known as mast, which is a source of food for several birds.

Oakwoods on heavy clay soils may have a shrub layer containing Hazel, Hawthorn, Holly, Bramble, Honeysuckle, Ivy and species of Rose. Other trees which may be present include Hornbeam, Aspen, Sallows, White Poplar, Elm, Wild Cherry and Service Tree. The field layer commonly contains Bluebell, Ground Ivy, Primrose, Wood Anemone and Wood Violet.

Beechwoods with a fairly open canopy may contain Elder, Spindle, Wild Privet and Dogwood. Those not growing on Clay-with-Flints may have an understorey of Yew. Dog's Mercury and Wood Sanicle are typical field layer plants.

Pinewoods are generally too dark and the soil too acid to contain much plant life. Furthermore, the layers of pine needles inhibit seed germination; they build up because bacteria, which normally decompose dead matter, avoid acidity.

▲ Hazel bushes are easily recognized by their nuts in autumn, and catkins (male flowers) in spring; female flowers appear as tiny red spikes.

▲ Twayblade (*left*) can be distinguished by its two large oval leaves; it occurs in grassland and scrub on the Downs as well as in woods. Wood Spurge (*centre*) oozes a white fluid when its stems are cut. Sanicle (*right*) may have pink or greenish-white flowers. All these plants favour chalk soils.

▼ Badgers are nocturnal, living in burrows by day. In spring, pieces of dead plants (old bedding) by holes are a sign of their presence.

▼ Roe Deer are most easily seen in the early morning when they emerge from woods to feed on grass; in summer their coat is orange-brown.

▲ The Brimstone Butterfly hibernates as an adult and may first emerge early in the year on warm February days.

▼ The Silver-washed Fritillary and White Admiral often feed on Bramble flowers. The Speckled Wood is well camouflaged in the dappled light of woodland glades.

Toadstools are often conspicuous in Pinewoods; like mushrooms, they are the fruiting or reproductive bodies of fungi. Fungi exist as a mass of tiny threads buried in soil, fallen leaves or wood. In Pinewoods they help to decompose pine needles but are less efficient agents of decomposition than bacteria. Less dense Pinewoods may harbour Birch trees, Gorse and in some places Bilberry.

Animal life in the woods is plentiful, though often well out of sight. Fallow Deer (locally), Roe Deer, Moles, Dormice, Badgers and Foxes are woodland animals, although Badgers are usually absent from heavy clay soils. The Grey Squirrel, introduced from America in the nineteenth century, has become a serious pest in woods, destroying young trees and eating the eggs and young of our native birds. In the South-East, the Red Squirrel is now to be seen only on the Isle of Wight where as yet there are no Grey Squirrels.

Several butterflies are common in woods in summer months. The Holly Blue visits Holly and Ivy flowers and lays its eggs on these plants. The Brimstone, White Admiral, Silver-washed Fritillary and Speckled Wood Butterfly may also be seen.

Woodland birds are more often heard than seen; typical species include Blue, Coal and Great Tits, Starling, Jay, Great-spotted, Green and Lesser-spotted Woodpeckers, Nuthatch, Treecreeper, Stock Dove, Woodpigeon, Blackbird, Song Thrush, Robin, Wren and Tawny Owl. Different types of woods attract different birds but the following migrants are found in most woods during the summer: Willow, Wood and Garden Warblers, Turtle Dove, Nightingale and Blackcap.

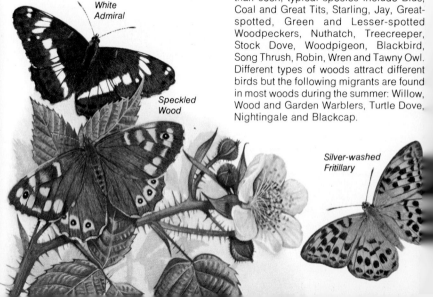

White Admiral

Speckled Wood

Silver-washed Fritillary

▲ The Hawfinch inhabits woodland and parks, especially where Beech and Hornbeam grow; it cracks fruit stones with its powerful bill.

▲ The Wood Warbler is a summer visitor, occuring mainly in semi-open Beech or Oakwoods. It builds its nest on the ground.

▲ The song of the Nightingale, a summer visitor, may be heard at night, as well as by day, in deciduous woods of the South-East.

▲ The Turtle Dove also visits Britain in summer; it may be seen on farmland and along hedgerows as well as in woodland.

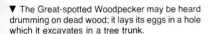

▼ The Great-spotted Woodpecker may be heard drumming on dead wood; it lays its eggs in a hole which it excavates in a tree trunk.

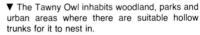

▼ The Tawny Owl inhabits woodland, parks and urban areas where there are suitable hollow trunks for it to nest in.

The Coast

Although South-East England is one of the most populated parts of the country and much of its coast is formalized into ports, seaside resorts and recreation beaches, there are still some valuable areas for wildlife. Several important habitats occur along the coast: saltmarshes with mudflats, maritime meadows, shingle, sand dunes and a few areas of cliffs.

Coastal areas, especially the saltmarshes and mudflats, are excellent sites for birdwatching throughout the year, but particularly in spring and autumn when many birds are migrating. In winter, birds from northern countries and other parts of Britain often collect in large numbers on the region's saltmarshes and mudflats.

The best time for birdwatching on the coast is when the low tide is on the turn and birds are pushed upshore by the incoming tide. Many species of wader come to feed along the shores, especially in winter. Some, like the Redshank, Black-tailed Godwit and Curlew have long bills and probe the sand and mud in search of worms and molluscs. The Turnstone has a short bill and turns over stones and seaweed to find food. The Sanderling, found mostly on sandy shores, may be seen running along the water's edge as it feeds. Other waders to look out for include Dunlin, Knot, Plovers, Sandpipers, Whimbrel and Oystercatcher. Ducks, geese, gulls and, in summer, terns can also be seen along the coast.

Several birds breed along the coast but many nesting sites have either disappeared, or have been so altered or disturbed as to no longer offer suitable places for some formerly regular breeders. Among those birds which have suffered most from loss of nesting sites in the South-East are the Sandwich Tern, Stone Curlew, Kentish Plover, Raven and Peregrine Falcon, which has also been adversely affected by pesticides.

Saltmarshes that are more or less inundated at high tide are obviously not suitable for breeding birds, but undisturbed areas of maritime meadow provide nest

▼ This view of the Seven Sisters, just west of Beachy Head, shows the purity of the chalk rock of the region. Chalk cliffs may also be seen between St Margaret's and Folkestone, and between Eastbourne and Brighton. A rich variety of chalk-loving plants often grows along these cliff tops.

cover for a number of species of duck and wader. Maritime meadows are normally situated behind sea walls and provide grazing for cattle. They commonly contain rank grass and occasionally rushes, sedges and beds of Common Reed. In those areas that are not heavily grazed, Mallard, Gadwall, Garganey, Pintail, Shoveler, Redshank and Snipe may nest.

Shingle and sand offer little protection to nesting birds. Lapwing, Ringed Plover, Common and Little Terns and Oyster-catcher breed in these habitats and pro-tect themselves to some extent by nesting in colonies. They make little in the way of a nest, often laying their well-camouflaged eggs into a simple hollow in the ground. The young have the ability to freeze when disturbed and afford some of the best examples of bird camouflage.

Apart from stretches of striking white cliffs composed of chalk, there are also a few areas of sandstone cliffs in the South-East – notably on the Isle of Wight and between Fairlight Cove and Hastings. Birds that breed in cliff areas include Jackdaw, Kestrel, Herring Gull (which also nests on shingle) and sometimes Lesser Black-backed Gull and Cormorant.

▲ Saltmarsh with Sea Purslane growing on the raised banks. Large areas of saltmarsh occur along the Thames Estuary and Hampshire Basin.

▲ Brent Geese are winter visitors; they may be seen along estuaries, on mudflats and occasion-ally in fields further inland.

▲ The smaller Black-headed Gull nests on dunes, shingle, marshes or islands in estuaries.

▼ The long-legged Black-tailed Godwit may be seen in winter along estuaries and by lakes.

▲ The Herring Gull is common on the coast all year round; its yellow bill has a red spot.

▼ Curlews breed on moorland but in winter may be seen on mudflats in the South-East.

Coastal plants are specially adapted to survive the drying effects of wind and salt. Many have thick leaves which store water, or leaves with a waxy covering that inhibits evaporation. Other coastal plants have long roots that enable them to reach sources of fresh water.

Each coastal habitat has its own characteristic flowers, although some species commonly occur in more than one habitat. Many coastal plants, such as Sea Aster and Sea Campion, are close relatives of inland plants. Sea Aster is a typical saltmarsh plant, often found growing with Sea Plantain, Sea Lavender and Annual Seablite. Glasswort may be abundant nearer the low tide mark, while higher up the shore Sea Purslane, Sea Wormwood, Sea Beet and, occasionally, Tamarisk grow.

Shingle beaches are much less extensive in the South-East than saltmarshes, except at Dungeness in Kent. Here, in some parts of this large area of shingle, are a number of common inland plants including Blackthorn, Bramble, Hawthorn, Elder, Evening Primrose, Holly and a prostrate form of Broom that avoids the buffeting of the wind.

Most shingle beaches are inhospitable habitats, yet some plants can survive. On unstable shingle, plants must grow very rapidly to keep pace with the shifting pebbles. On more stable shingle, organic matter eventually accumulates between the pebbles, and plants such as Sea Beet, Sea Kale, Yellow Horned Poppy and Yellow Stonecrop can take root. Plants that occur on any well-drained soil, such as Mouse-ear Hawkweed and Viper's Bugloss, may also be found on shingle.

To most people, sandy beaches and dunes are more attractive than shingle, if only for greater comfort underfoot. Dunes vary in height according to their age and history. Marram Grass and Sand Couch-grass are the most conspicuous of plants that help to stabilize and build up the dunes. Other typical plants are Sea Holly, Sea Rocket, Sea Sandwort and Sea Spurge. The prickly Burnet Rose usually grows on older, more stable dunes, sometimes together with Sea Buckthorn.

Cliff plants are affected by salt spray, and may be either specially salt-tolerant species or plants that are widespread inland but able to tolerate some salt. The large-leaved Alexanders grows anywhere near the coast but is particularly noticeable along cliffs. Other cliff plants include Rock Samphire, Wild Cabbage, Thrift and Fennel whose leaves smell of aniseed when crushed.

Many butterflies are attracted to coastal plants; in summer the Painted Lady and Clouded Yellow, two species which migrate from the Continent, may first be seen along stretches of the south coast.

▲ Sea Purslane, a grey-green shrubby plant with tiny yellowish flowers in July and August, grows around salty pools and creeks in saltmarshes.

▼ Sea Kale, a distinctive plant of shingle and sand, has large cabbage-like leaves and clusters of white flowers from June to August.

▼ Golden Samphire, with Dandelion-like flowers in July and August, grows in saltmarshes near the high tide mark, and occasionally on cliffs.

▲ Yellow Horned Poppy (*left*) grows on shingle; its thin curved seed pods may be 30 cm long. Alexanders (*centre*) is a robust plant, up to 130 cm high, with yellowish flowers. Sea Buckthorn (*right*) is a thorny shrub often planted to stabilize dunes. Only the female plants bear orange berries.

▼ Marram, Sea Holly, Sea Spurge and Sea Rocket are amongst the first plants to colonize sand dunes. The Clouded Yellow Butterfly may be seen along the coast, having just completed its migratory flight across the Channel.

Ringed Plover

Marram Grass

Sea Holly

Clouded Yellow Butterfly

Sea Spurge

Sea Rocket

Heathland

Heathland is similar to moorland in that both areas have an acid soil containing few nutrients. Moors are found mainly in damp upland areas, generally in the north and west of Britain; heaths occur in drier lowland areas on sandy soils. Heathland supports a very characteristic vegetation including Heathers, Gorse, Silver Birch and Scots Pine.

The most extensive areas of heath in the South-East occur in south-west Surrey, in the Ashdown Forest and in the New Forest. Despite their natural appearance, the southern heathlands, like the Chalk Downs, are very much man-made.

Centuries ago, areas of the original forests were cleared so that the light sandy soils could be cultivated. Without the annual leaf fall there was no humus to enrich the soil, and once the soil was exhausted, man simply cleared further areas of forest to grow more crops. The abandoned land was washed through by rain, which drains easily through sandy soil, and most of the remaining nutrients

were therefore washed away. Later, only those plants that could grow in an acid and impoverished soil were able to colonize these areas.

Much of the vegetation of open heaths consists of Bell Heather, whose leaves stand out from the stem at right angles, and its close relative, Ling, distinguished by its tiny leaves that grow flat against the stem. Bilberry, a low-growing shrub, is widely distributed, especially on higher ground. Two species of gorse are also typical heathland plants; the yellow flowers of the common Gorse are conspicuous from early spring until June when its smaller relative, Dwarf Gorse, begins to flower. On a hot sunny day in July the seed pods of Gorse can be heard popping in the heat. The seeds are shot out, sometimes along with a tiny beetle which has undergone its life cycle in the pod. Here and there in early summer the yellow flowers of Broom can be found. Bracken, a type of fern, is almost ubiquitous and is a sure indicator of an acid soil. Birch trees and Scots Pine

▼ Typical open heathland of the South-East with characteristic plants: Bracken, Bell Heather and Ling growing together in the foreground and conifer trees in the distance.

are common on this kind of soil, while the Sessile Oak or its hybrid with the English Oak, grows on richer heathland soils.

Sheep's Sorrel, with its small, often reddish spear-like leaves, may be found along open paths. In damper places, dense isolated tufts of Heath Rush occur along with Cross-leaved Heather, which can be distinguished from other heathers by its pale pink globular flowers, and leaves which grow in groups of four.

Most heathland areas contain boggy patches with a specialized flora, including several species of *Sphagnum* moss, Deer Grass, Whitebeaked Sedge and the insectivorous Sundews. Apart from the possible danger to the walker, the vegetation is very vulnerable to damage when trodden upon, so these boggy areas should be carefully avoided, except where a nature trail has been laid out.

Comparatively few small animals are found on heaths, largely owing to the dry soil and limited number of plant species available as food. The soil is deficient in calcium, which is necessary for shell formation and consequently snails are rare. Heather Beetles and Honey Bees are common but the number of different kinds of insects is small compared with that of the chalklands.

The Common Lizard and Adder inhabit heaths. Linnets, Sand Martins (in summer) and Tree Pipits are among the commoner birds to be seen in these areas. Stonechats also occur and Nightjars may be seen in summer on Bracken-covered heaths. Typical butterflies include the Silver-studded Blue and the Grayling. The Emperor Moth flies over heathland in early summer, and its caterpillar may be seen on Ling.

The Nightjar is more often heard than seen; its churring call, somewhat like a motorbike in the distance, is most frequent at dusk.

▲ The Silver-studded Blue inhabits heathland, mainly in southern England. The uppersides of the wings are blue (male) or brown (female).

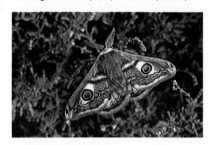
▲ The male Emperor Moth is active by day in April and May on heaths.

▼ The Emperor Moth caterpillar blends in well with Ling, one of its food plants.

▼ The Stonechat frequents Gorse-covered heaths. The male (not shown) has a black head with white neck patches and a red breast.

▲ On warm days the Common Lizard may be seen on heaths, basking in the sun. When threatened, it can cast off its tail, then – like the lizard shown here has done – grow a new one.

▲ Cotton Grass grows in damp boggy places. Its fluffy white seed heads may be seen in June and early July. The white "cotton" is too coarse to be spun into thread.

▲ Bilberry, a small shrub with green stems, bears pink flowers from April to June, and edible black berries in August and September.

▼ Bog Asphodel, a typical plant of boggy areas, flowers in July and August; its leaves resemble those of an iris and are often curved.

▲ Broom resembles Gorse but has no spines; its bright yellow flowers can be seen on heathland in May and June.

▼ The Common Sundew traps insects on its sticky red leaves and then digests them. It grows in bogs and flowers between June and August.

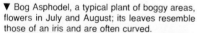

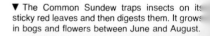

The New Forest

The New Forest, like the Ashdown Forest of East Sussex, is by no means uniformly wooded and contains considerable areas of open heathland. The whole of the 25,900 hectares (about 100 square miles) comprises one of the most extensive areas of semi-natural vegetation in lowland Britain. The Forest is an attractive mixture of heathland, which is covered in some areas with Ling and in others with Gorse, and woodland of all ages. There is a little cultivated land, and also some grazing meadows, usually as clearings beside streams.

The New Forest was set aside by the Normans for hunting, especially deer. Clearance of the Forest and hunting by commoners was strictly forbidden, though certain rights to graze and take wood were granted. In later years, the Forest was used more as a valuable source of timber than for hunting. Today timber production is still very important in the New Forest and the area is largely under the control of the Forestry Commission. A number of nature reserves exist within the Forest, and visitors are asked to observe carefully the bye-laws designed to protect the Forest and its wildlife. Car parks and other amenities are provided.

The woods of the New Forest are varied; there are old Oak forests with some Beeches as well as more recent plantations. Half of the plantations consist of conifers, mostly Scots Pine, but also a number of non-native evergreens like the Douglas Fir, European Larch and Sitka Spruce.

A typical New Forest scene with Scots Pine and open dry heath. Fields and mixed planted woodland can be seen in the distance.

▲ Fallow Deer have distinct dappled markings; the bucks have flattened antlers and should never be approached during the rutting season, in autumn, as they may attack people.

▲ The New Forest ponies roam more or less free through the Forest; they are owned by local people who have special grazing rights.

▼ An old pollarded Beech – cut down to about three metres many years ago, it now has several major trunks instead of one.

▲ Large Marsh Grasshopper on Bog Myrtle fruit – this insect lives in damp areas of the Forest.

▲ The Long-eared Owl lives mainly in woods; it often uses another bird's old nest.

▲ The Hobby, a summer visitor to southern England, may be seen in open woodland of the New Forest.

▲ The Crossbill (male shown here) occurs in pinewoods of the New Forest, mainly in winter. The female is olive-green.

▲ The Redstart, a summer visitor to Britain, constantly flicks its orange tail; it may be seen in open woods, parkland and ruins.

▲ The rare Dartford Warbler, a long-tailed bird inhabits heaths where it usually nests in Gorse bushes.

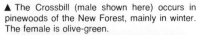

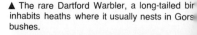

Other plantations contain broadleaved trees, mainly Oak and Beech. The conifer woods generally occur on more acid soils and are often too dark for plants to grow in. As plants are fundamental to animal life, these woods support a more limited range of insects, birds and mammals than the broadleaved woods.

Deer still inhabit the Forest; Roe and Fallow are the most common and there are also a few Red Deer and the introduced Japanese Sika. In the past overgrazing by deer, ponies, cattle and pigs damaged the trees preventing new growth of wood needed for timber. Instead of being coppiced (see page 18) young trees were therefore pollarded – that is cut down to a height of about three metres – so that the new shoots which grew from the cut trunk were out of reach of browsing animals. It has also been the practice since the eighteenth century, again for the purposes of timber production, to protect trees from grazing animals by enclosing certain areas. These enclosures are richer in wildlife than the open areas, which are often heavily grazed by the New Forest ponies.

Bog Myrtle is very much a New Forest bush. It grows along woodland edges and in other damp places; the Heath-spotted Orchid is often found in similar places. Many other plants of heathland and woodland (see pages 18 and 26) also grow in the New Forest. Rhododendron, an introduced species, now grows wild in the Forest. Although an attractive shrub when in flower, it spreads rapidly in dense thickets and chokes out other plant growth.

Holly, Rowan and Yew are common in the Forest and their winter berries provide food for birds, especially the Fieldfare and Redwing. Since the Forest has seen little formal game-rearing, the larger birds of prey have suffered less from shooting than in most parts of the country. There is a reasonable chance of seeing Buzzard, Sparrowhawk, Kestrel and, in summer, the Hobby. The Long-eared Owl may be seen in wooded areas while Tawny, Barn and Little Owls occur more frequently along woodland edges.

The Nightjar is found in heathland Bracken and in woodland rides. The Woodlark, Stonechat, Meadow Pipit, Linnet, Long-tailed Tit and rare Dartford Warbler also inhabit heathland areas of the Forest.

The white-faced Barn Owl hunts by night for mice and other small animals. During the day it roosts in a dark place such as an old tree, or sometimes a barn or church tower.

▼ The Heath-spotted Orchid grows on acid soils; like the Common Spotted Orchid, it has spotted leaves but can be distinguished by the frilled edges to the outer lobes of the flower lip.

Other birds to look out for in the wooded areas are Hawfinch, Crossbill, Redpoll, Redstart, Goldcrest, all three species of woodpecker and, in summer, Wood and Willow Warblers and Chiffchaff. In recent years, the rare Firecrest, which occurs in very limited numbers in southern England, has bred in the New Forest, mainly in coniferous woods.

The Forest abounds with many kinds of insect: some are typical heathland and woodland species, but others are quite rare and at least one species, the New Forest Cicada, occurs only in the New Forest. The Pearl-bordered and Small Pearl-bordered Fritillaries and Speckled Wood Butterfly may all be seen during the summer months, and in late summer, the continuous chirruping of the Wood Cricket may be heard in some places.

On more open heathland areas the Adder may be seen and in a few places the rare Sand Lizard and harmless Smooth Snake still occur. The Sand Lizard is larger than the Common Lizard and can be distinguished by the rows of dark spots with white centres that run down its back. The Smooth Snake is grey or brown with a darker head and a series of darker spots along its body. Both reptiles are confined to a few sandy areas in southern England.

▼ The New Forest Cicada occurs only in the New Forest; it has transparent wings and is relatively large – about 25 mm long.

▲ The Sand Lizard occurs infrequently on som dry heaths; the male has greenish flanks.

▲ The Smooth Snake often occurs in the san areas as the Sand Lizard, which it preys on.

▲ Male Purple Emperor Butterfly – though ra this species is now increasing in numbers; inhabits woods where Goat Willow grows.

▼ The Pearl-bordered Fritillary may be seen woodland in May and June. The male (not shov is similar but has less dark wing edges.

Common Species of the Countryside and Seashore

Some of Britain's animals and plants can be found only in certain regions, or are more easily found in some areas than in others. Living alongside these rare or local species are, of course, many animals and plants which are fairly widespread throughout the country. The more common species of British birds, wild flowers, trees, butterflies, mammals and seashore animals are illustrated on the following pages. These illustrations form a basic field guide to the majority of the regions in Britain.

The captions to the bird illustrations indicate the bird's usual haunts, and if it is seen only in certain seasons, this fact is mentioned. Measurements indicate the size of the bird from the tip of the beak to the end of the tail. Notes to aid identification of the species are also included.

The mammals that are illustrated are accompanied by captions which indicate their average size. Those for hoofed mammals indicate their height at the shoulder. Others indicate the length of their bodies from nose to rump. The captions also give an indication as to when the animal is most active and therefore most easily observed.

The wild flowers are grouped according to their commonest colours; their most frequently used names are given in the captions, along with their habitats, the months in which they flower and their height or the length of creeping stems if they grow horizontally.

The illustrations of butterflies frequently show them on the plants they prefer to visit. The captions indicate the butterflies' usual habitats, the months when they are most frequently seen, and their wingspan.

Information about the sizes of the seashore animals are detailed in their captions, while the height of the trees is given on page 96. Selected identifying characteristics are given in the captions to the trees.

A hedgerow in early summer—one of the countryside's most rewarding habitats, since it shelters a wide variety of species. This illustration features some of the common, widespread plants and animals included in the following pages.

Birds

Canada Goose ▶
Fields and marshes near water; parks. Brown wings and body. Introduced from Canada. 95 cm.

Shag ▶
Rocky coats, where it nests in colonies. Has crest only in breeding season. Flies low, close to the water. 78 cm.

Cormorant ▶
Near the sea and some large inland waters. Has white thigh patch in breeding season. Larger than Shag. 92 cm.

Spring

◀ Mute Swan
Wide rivers, lakes, tow parks. Not, as its nam implies, mute. Britain' most common swan. 152 cm.

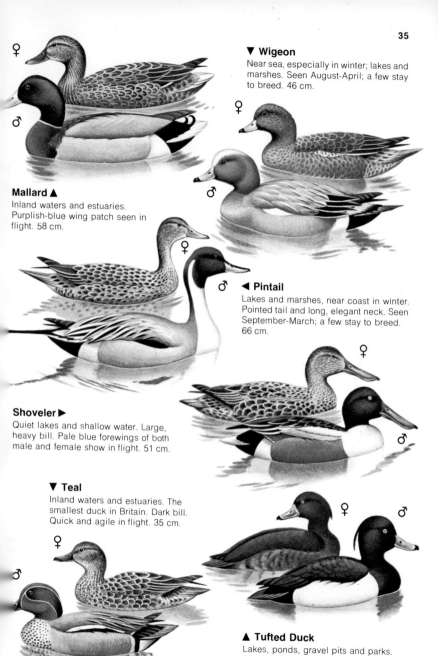

▼ Wigeon

Near sea, especially in winter; lakes and marshes. Seen August-April; a few stay to breed. 46 cm.

Mallard ▲

Inland waters and estuaries. Purplish-blue wing patch seen in flight. 58 cm.

◀ Pintail

Lakes and marshes, near coast in winter. Pointed tail and long, elegant neck. Seen September-March; a few stay to breed. 66 cm.

Shoveler ▶

Quiet lakes and shallow water. Large, heavy bill. Pale blue forewings of both male and female show in flight. 51 cm.

▼ Teal

Inland waters and estuaries. The smallest duck in Britain. Dark bill. Quick and agile in flight. 35 cm.

▲ Tufted Duck

Lakes, ponds, gravel pits and parks. Dumpy, active diving duck. Note female's yellow eye. 43 cm.

▼ Pochard
Lakes and backwaters. In flight, both sexes have dark wings with paler grey central bar. 46 cm.

▲ Shelduck
Coasts and estuaries, often in flocks; also large inland lakes. Female has no red knob on bill. 61 cm.

▲ Red-breasted Merganser
Coastal areas; wooded lakes, rivers, in breeding season. 58 cm.

Grey Heron ▶
Near water: rivers, lakes and seashores. Head is drawn back in flight. 92 cm.

Summer

Winter

▼ Little Grebe
Inland waters. Secretive and hard to spot. 27 cm.

▲ Great Crested Grebe
Inland waters, sometimes on sea in winter. 48 cm.

Winter

Summer

Buzzard ▼
Often seen soaring over moors
and farmland. Rare in east and
south-east England. 54 cm.

▼ Kestrel
Moors, coasts, farmland;
some nest in towns.
Hovers when hunting.
34 cm.

Coot ▶
Lakes, reservoirs,
open water.
Larger, heavier
bird than
Moorhen.
38 cm.

▲ Moorhen
Ponds, lakes and streams. 33 cm.

◀ Partridge
Farmland, moors. Small head,
short tail and legs. Often in
small groups. 30 cm.

♂

▼ Pheasant
Farmland, scrub,
woodland. Males can
have white neckring.
Male 87 cm, female
58 cm.

♀

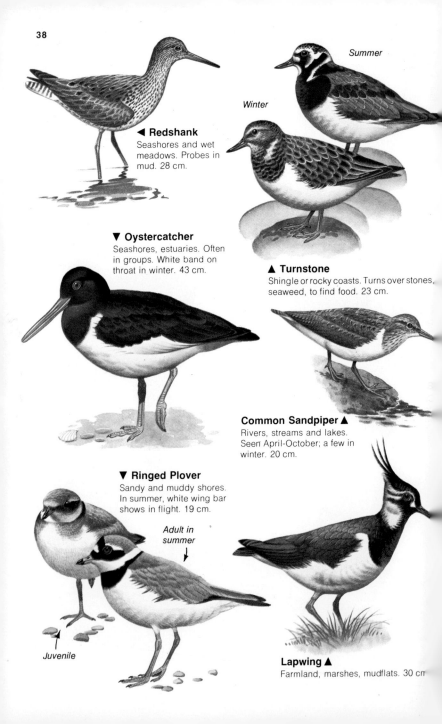

◀ Redshank
Seashores and wet
meadows. Probes in
mud. 28 cm.

Summer

Winter

▼ Oystercatcher
Seashores, estuaries. Often
in groups. White band on
throat in winter. 43 cm.

▲ Turnstone
Shingle or rocky coasts. Turns over stones,
seaweed, to find food. 23 cm.

Common Sandpiper ▲
Rivers, streams and lakes.
Seen April-October; a few in
winter. 20 cm.

▼ Ringed Plover
Sandy and muddy shores.
In summer, white wing bar
shows in flight. 19 cm.

*Adult in
summer*

Juvenile

Lapwing ▲
Farmland, marshes, mudflats. 30 cm

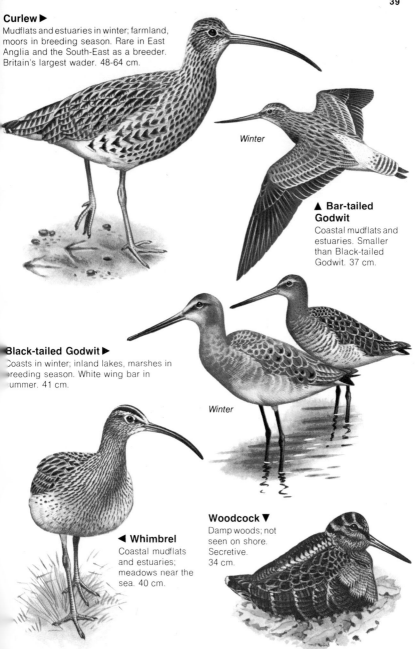

Curlew ▶

Mudflats and estuaries in winter; farmland, moors in breeding season. Rare in East Anglia and the South-East as a breeder. Britain's largest wader. 48-64 cm.

Winter

▲ Bar-tailed Godwit

Coastal mudflats and estuaries. Smaller than Black-tailed Godwit. 37 cm.

Black-tailed Godwit ▶

Coasts in winter; inland lakes, marshes in breeding season. White wing bar in summer. 41 cm.

Winter

◀ Whimbrel

Coastal mudflats and estuaries; meadows near the sea. 40 cm.

Woodcock ▼

Damp woods; not seen on shore. Secretive. 34 cm.

Snipe ▼
Wet fields, marshes or lake
edges. Probes while
standing still. 27 cm.

Winter

Summer

▲ Dunlin
Mudflats and estuaries. Common winter
shorebird; less common in summer. 19 cm.

Greenshank ▼
Coasts, marshes. Seen chiefly on
migration. Some breed in Scotland. 30 cm.

Winter

▲ Sanderling
Sandy shores along coasts. Seen
August-May. Short, straight beak. 20 cm.

Summer

◄ Ruff
Marshes, wet
meadows, edges
of reservoirs.
Seen mostly in
spring and
autumn. 29 cm.

♂

♂

Winter

▼ Knot
Sand or mudflats in
estuaries. Larger tha
Dunlin. Seen mostly
August-May. 25 cm.

Winter

▼ Common Tern
Near sea; also nests inland in Scotland.
Seen April-October. 34 cm.

Summer

Summer

◀ Little Tern
Shingle beaches. Never
has full black cap like other
terns. Seen
April-September. 24 cm.

Herring Gull ▼
Coastal ports and seaside
towns. Wingtips are black
with white spots. 56 cm.

◀ Black-headed Gull
Inland and near the sea. Dark
brown "hood" in summer
only. 37 cm.

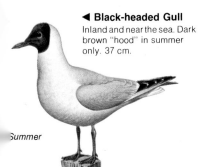

Summer

Summer

Common Gull ▶
Coasts; often inland in
winter. Smaller and
less widespread than
Herring Gull. 41 cm.

Lesser
Black-backed
Gull ▶
Coasts and inland.
Mainly a summer
visitor. 53 cm.

42

▼ Guillemot
Rocky coasts. Neck and throat are white in winter. Seen at cliff sites December-August. 42 cm.

◄ Fulmar
Rocky coasts. Nests on cliffs. Always sits, never stands. Mostly out at sea in winter. 47 cm.

Puffin ►
Rocky islands and sea cliffs. Colourful bill in summer. 30 cm.

Summer

Summer

▼ Collared Dove
Large gardens, parks and farmland. Long white tail with black base. 30 cm

◄ Stock Dove
Woods and cliffs; sometimes in towns. Darker, smaller bird tha Woodpigeon. 33 cm.

Rock Dove ▼
Coasts, usually on sea cliffs. Town pigeons are descended from these birds. 33 cm.

Woodpigeon ►
Farmland, woods and towns. White neck patch on adult. 41 cm.

▼ Short-eared Owl
Open country. Hunts in day-time or at dusk. 37 cm.

◀ Barn Owl
Open country, especially farmland. Mostly nocturnal. 34 cm.

◀ Long-eared Owl
Edges of woods. Underside all dark. Nocturnal. 34 cm.

Little Owl ▼
Farmland and wooded country. Underside is streaked. Often seen in daylight. 22 cm.

▲ Tawny Owl
Parks, woodland and farmland; sometimes towns. Large head. Nocturnal. 38 cm.

◀ Kingfisher
Near rivers and lakes; seashore in winter. Dives from low perch or from a hover. 17 cm.

▼ Cuckoo
Anywhere in countryside. Male's song is well known. April-September. 30 cm.

Swift ▶
Breeds mainly in towns;
may fly over countryside.
Seen end of April-
August/September. 17 cm.

▼ Sand Martin
Banks and sandy cliffs. Seen
April-September. 12 cm.

◀ House Martin
Suburban areas and
countryside. Seen
April-October.
13 cm.

◀ Swallow
Farms and open country
often near water. Seen
April-September/October
19 cm.

**◀ Great Spotted
Woodpecker**
Woodlands. Large
white patches on
wings. 23 cm.

**◀ Green
Woodpecker**
Deciduous woods
parks. Yellow-gre
rump seen in fligh
Rare in Scotland.
32 cm.

**Lesser Spotted
Woodpecker ▶**
Deciduous woods,
parks. Not in
Scotland.
Sparrow-sized.
14 cm.

▼ Dunnock
Bushes and shrubs everywhere.
Slender bill, unlike sparrows. 14.5 cm.

▲ Meadow Pipit
Upland moors and other open areas. .
Smaller, daintier than larks. 14.5 cm.

Tree Pipit ▲
Heaths and areas with
scattered trees. Seen
April-September. 15 cm.

▲ Skylark
Open country, especially farmland.
Rises vertically to a great height in song
flight. 18 cm.

**◄ Yellow
Wagtail**
Grassy places
near water.
Seen April-late
September.
17 cm.

♂

Summer

◄ Grey Wagtail
By lochs or
fast-flowing hill
steams;
waterfalls in
lowlands. 18 cm.

▲ Pied Wagtail
Towns and countryside, usually near
water. Females are greyer. Takes insects
from the ground or the air. 18 cm.

▼ Willow Warbler
Gardens, woods and hedgerows. Flatter head and longer tail than Chiffchaff. Seen April-September. 11 cm.

▲ Sedge Warbler
Thick vegetation near water. Broad, pale stripe over eye. Seen April-September. 13 cm.

Wren ▶
Towns and countryside. Tiny, rotund bird with cocked tail. 9.5 cm.

Reed Warbler ▼
Reed beds. Not in Scotland. Seen April-September. 13 cm.

♂

♀

▲ Blackcap
Wooded areas. Seen April-September, a few in winter. 14 cm.

▼ Whitethroat
Thick, low bushes. Seen April-September. 14 cm.

▲ Garden Warbler
Hedges or woods with thick under-growth. Seen April-September. 14 cm.

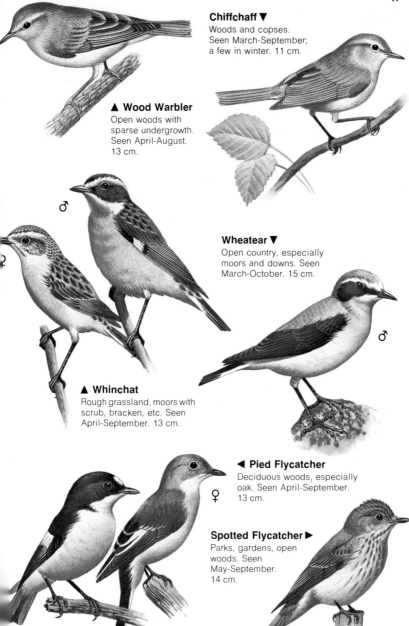

Chiffchaff ▼
Woods and copses.
Seen March-September;
a few in winter. 11 cm.

▲ Wood Warbler
Open woods with
sparse undergrowth.
Seen April-August.
13 cm.

♂

♀

Wheatear ▼
Open country, especially
moors and downs. Seen
March-October. 15 cm.

♂

▲ Whinchat
Rough grassland, moors with
scrub, bracken, etc. Seen
April-September. 13 cm.

◄ Pied Flycatcher
Deciduous woods, especially
oak. Seen April-September.
13 cm.

♀

Spotted Flycatcher ▶
Parks, gardens, open
woods. Seen
May-September.
14 cm.

Blackbird ▼
In trees and bushes everywhere.
Young are paler than female
with breast more strongly
spotted. 25 cm.

♀

♂

▼ Starling
Most places, including cities. In
summer, has purple and green
gloss and mostly yellow bill.
22 cm.

Juvenile

*Adult
in
winter*

▲ Redwing
Farmland, commons and
other open areas. A few breed in
Scotland. Seen October-April. 21 cm.

◀ Fieldfare
Farmland,
orchards, open
areas. White
underwings.
Seen
October-April.
25.5 cm.

▼ Redstart
Heaths, parks, open woods. Seen
April-September. Rather Robin-like.
14 cm.

♀

♂

Robin ▲
Gardens, hedgerows and
woodland. Juvenile is spotted,
without any red. 14 cm.

◄ Song Thrush
Trees and bushes in towns and country.
Smashes snails on stones. 23 cm.

Long-tailed Tit ►
Hedgerows and
woodland edges.
14 cm. (7.5 cm of
which is the tail).

◄ Great Tit
Gardens and
woodlands. Black
band on chest. 14 cm.

◄ Blue Tit
Woods and gardens.
Dark line on belly.
11 cm.

▲ Mistle Thrush
Woodland and open areas.
Larger than Blackbird; paler,
greyer than Song Thrush. 27 cm.

▼ Marsh Tit
Deciduous woods;
infrequently in
gardens. 11 cm.

▲ Coal Tit
Coniferous woods, parks,
gardens. Oblong white patch
on nape. 11 cm.

▼ Chaffinch
Farmland, hedgerows and
woodland. Male is duller in winter.
White wing bar seen in flight.
15 cm.

♀

♂

▲ Siskin
Usually coniferous woods in
summer; birch, alder woods,
sometimes gardens, in winter. 11 cm.

♀

♂

Summer

▲ Nuthatch
Deciduous wood and parks. Can
descend trees head-first. Very
short tail. Rare in Scotland.
14 cm.

▲ Hawfinch
Deciduous woodland,
orchards. Very elusive. Big
head and massive, broad
bill. 16 cm.

◄ Treecreeper
Woodland, sometimes parks
and gardens. Creeps up tree
trunks using tail as support. 13 cm.

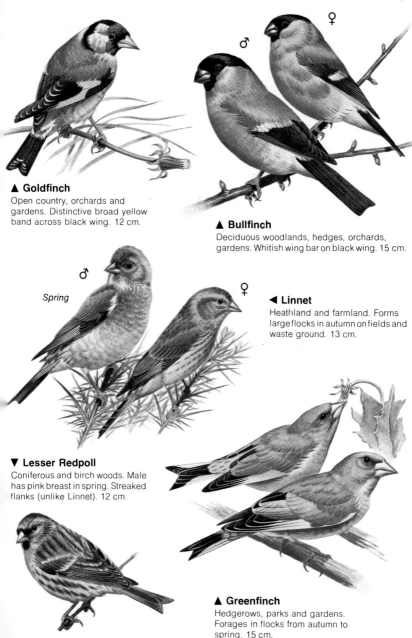

51

▲ Goldfinch
Open country, orchards and
gardens. Distinctive broad yellow
band across black wing. 12 cm.

▲ Bullfinch
Deciduous woodlands, hedges, orchards,
gardens. Whitish wing bar on black wing. 15 cm.

Spring

◀ Linnet
Heathland and farmland. Forms
large flocks in autumn on fields and
waste ground. 13 cm.

▼ Lesser Redpoll
Coniferous and birch woods. Male
has pink breast in spring. Streaked
flanks (unlike Linnet). 12 cm.

▲ Greenfinch
Hedgerows, parks and gardens.
Forages in flocks from autumn to
spring. 15 cm.

▼ Tree Sparrow
Farmland. White cheeks with black spot. Sometimes flocks with House Sparrow in winter. 14 cm.

▲ House Sparrow
Near houses in cities; on farms in the country. Distinctive black bib on male. 15 cm.

▲ Corn Bunting
Open country, especially cornfields. Bigger than other buntings and finches. 18 cm.

▲ Yellowhammer
Farmland, heaths, young plantations. Flocks forage in field in winter. Rare in Wales. 17 cm.

▲ Goldcrest
Large gardens and woods, especially conifers. Smallest British bird. 9 cm.

▲ Reed Bunting
Vegetation near water; may visit bird tables in winter. Male has less black on head in winter. 15 cm.

Carrion Crow ▶
Open country, town, along
coasts. Usually seen alone, in
pairs or small groups.
47 cm.

▼ Jay
Woodlands, parks and gardens.
White rump and blue wing flash
show in flight. 32 cm.

◀ Magpie
Hedgerows, farmland, scrub. Large
black and white bird. Long, slender
tail. 46 cm.

▼ Jackdaw
Cliffs, farmland and towns.
Small black and grey crow.
Forms large flocks. 33 cm.

▲ Rook
Farmland, open copses, villages. Forms
large flocks. Baggy thighs. Bare whitish
face in adults. 46 cm.

Mammals

▼ Red Fox
Farmland and woods, sometimes mountains and towns. Mainly nocturnal. 65 cm.

▲ Badger
Woods, sometimes mountains. Nocturnal. Can stay underground for several days in cold weather without food. 80 cm.

▼ Roe Deer
Conifer plantations, especially near water. Mainly nocturnal; hides during day. 70 cm.

▲ Hedgehog
Hedgerows, ditches, parks, gardens and moorland. Mainly nocturnal. 25 cm. .

▲ Mole
Underground in most kinds of soil in farmland, woods. Lives alone. Can swim well. 13 cm.

▼ Grey Squirrel
Woods, parks and gardens.
Introduced from N. America.
Diurnal. 27 cm.

Red Squirrel ▲
Mainly conifer woods. Partly replaced
by Grey Squirrel in England. 23 cm.

▼ Rabbit
Farmland, woodland, sand
dunes and hillsides. Active
at dusk and dawn. 40 cm.

◄ Brown Hare
Open farmland and
woodland. Mainly
nocturnal, but can often be
seen in day. 58 cm.

▼ Wood Mouse
Gardens,
hedgerows,
woods. Mainly
nocturnal. 9 cm.

▼ Common Shrew
Rough pasture, woods,
hedgerows, dunes and
marshes. Active day and
night. 7 cm.

▼ Short-tailed Vole
Open ground with
rough grass. Most
active at night; also
seen in day. 11 cm.

56

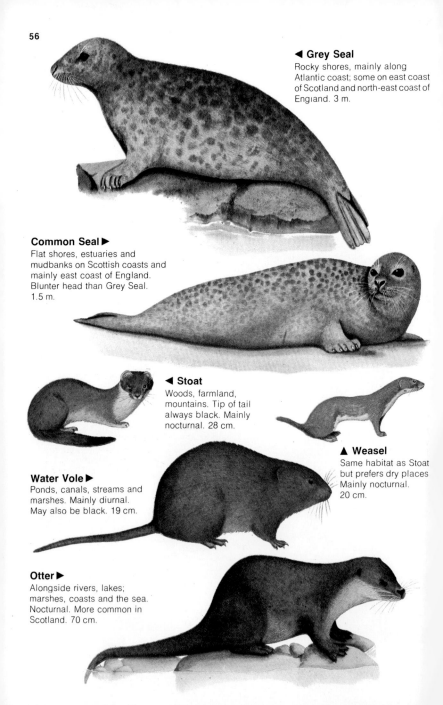

◄ Grey Seal
Rocky shores, mainly along
Atlantic coast; some on east coast
of Scotland and north-east coast of
England. 3 m.

Common Seal ▶
Flat shores, estuaries and
mudbanks on Scottish coasts and
mainly east coast of England.
Blunter head than Grey Seal.
1.5 m.

◄ Stoat
Woods, farmland,
mountains. Tip of tail
always black. Mainly
nocturnal. 28 cm.

▲ Weasel
Same habitat as Stoat
but prefers dry places
Mainly nocturnal.
20 cm.

Water Vole ▶
Ponds, canals, streams and
marshes. Mainly diurnal.
May also be black. 19 cm.

Otter ▶
Alongside rivers, lakes;
marshes, coasts and the sea.
Nocturnal. More common in
Scotland. 70 cm.

Wild Flowers

▼ Common St John's Wort
Damp, grassy places, open
woods, hedgebanks. Less
common in some northern areas.
June-September. 30-90 cm.

▲ Lesser Celandine
Damp, shady woods, grassy banks
and waysides. Creeping stems.
March-May. 5-25 cm.

◄ Bulbous Buttercup
Dry, grassy places. Base of stem is
swollen and bulb-like.
March-June. 15-40 cm.

▼ Cowslip
Meadows, pastures,
woods, copses. Absent
from much of Scotland.
April-May. 10-30 cm.

▼ Creeping Buttercup
Damp grassy places, woods,
gardens. Long, leafy, creeping
runners. May-August. Runners
15-60 cm.

▼ Creeping Jenny
Grassy, shady places; damp meadows,
woods, under hedges. Rare in northern
Scotland. June-August. Stems up to 60 cm.

◄ Yellow Rattle
Waysides and other grassy
places. Seeds rattle inside ripe
capsule. May-August. 12-40 cm.

Common Rockrose ►
Grassy, rocky places. Not a rose.
Leaves are hairy.
May-September 5-30 cm.

Aaron's Rod ►
Banks, waste places, open
scrub. Rarer in Scotland.
June-August. 30-200 cm.

◄ Groundsel
Waste places; a
common garden weed.
Flowers all year round.
8-45 cm.

▲ Primrose
Woods, hedges and fields. Rarer
in the North. February-May.
8-15 cm.

◄ Herb Bennet
Woods, hedges, shady places.
Fruits are hooked. June-August.
20-60 cm.

◄ Broom
Heaths, waste ground,
open woods,
scrubland. May-June.
60-200 cm.

▲ Yellow Pimpernel
Woods and shady
hedgebanks. May-September.
Trailing stems up to 40 cm long.

60

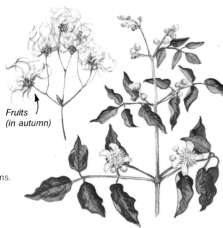

◀ Silverweed
Hedgebanks, grassy
places. Creeping stems.
May-August.

▲ Old Man's Beard
Woodland edges, hedgerows, scrub.
Rare in Scotland and northern
England. July-August. Up to 30 m.

*Fruits
(in autumn)*

▼ Bird's Foot Trefoil
Open, grassy places. Very long,
creeping stems. Pods look like a
bird's foot. May-June.

Golden Rod ▶
Woods, cliffs, hedges. Rarer
in the South-East.
July-September. 5-75 cm.

**▼ Creeping
Cinquefoil**
Hedgebanks, grassy
places. Creeping
stems. May-August.

▼ Ragwort

Roadsides, waste ground, grassy places. Flowerheads in flat-topped clusters. June-October. 30-150 cm

▲ Dandelion

Open grassy places and waste ground. March-October. 15-30 cm.

Rape ▶

Roadsides and fields. May-August. Up to 1m.

▼ Gorse

Heaths and commons. March-July. 60-200 cm.

▲ Wild Pansy

Grassy places and cornfields. Flowers can also be all yellow, all violet, or pink and white. April-September. 15-45 cm.

▼ Viper's Bugloss
Waysides and sand dunes. Sharp hairs on stems. Bristly leaves. Rare in Scotland. June-September. 30-90 cm.

Common Forget-me-Not ▶
Roadsides, fields, and open grassy places. April-September. 15-30 cm.

◀ Sea Aster
Saltmarshes. Petals can also be white. July-October. 1 m.

◀ Common Speedwell
Grassy places and woods. May-August. 10-40 cm.

Common Milkwort ▶
Heaths, dunes, grassy places. May-September. 10-30 cm.

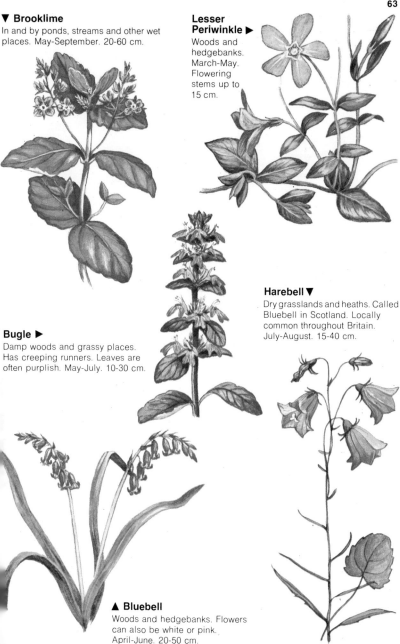

▼ Brooklime
In and by ponds, streams and other wet places. May-September. 20-60 cm.

Lesser Periwinkle ▶
Woods and hedgebanks. March-May. Flowering stems up to 15 cm.

Harebell ▼
Dry grasslands and heaths. Called Bluebell in Scotland. Locally common throughout Britain. July-August. 15-40 cm.

Bugle ▶
Damp woods and grassy places. Has creeping runners. Leaves are often purplish. May-July. 10-30 cm.

▲ Bluebell
Woods and hedgebanks. Flowers can also be white or pink. April-June. 20-50 cm.

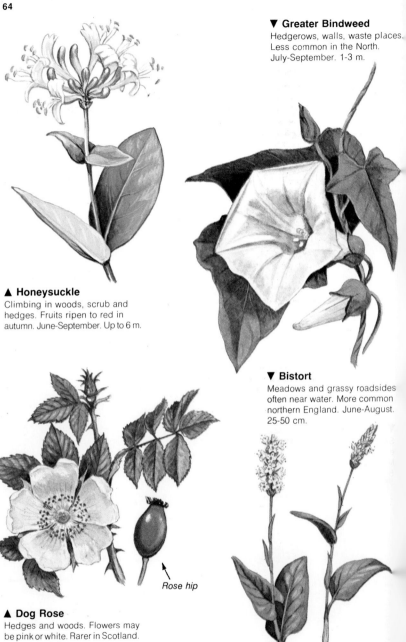

▼ Greater Bindweed
Hedgerows, walls, waste places. Less common in the North. July-September. 1-3 m.

▲ Honeysuckle
Climbing in woods, scrub and hedges. Fruits ripen to red in autumn. June-September. Up to 6 m.

▼ Bistort
Meadows and grassy roadsides often near water. More common northern England. June-August. 25-50 cm.

Rose hip

▲ Dog Rose
Hedges and woods. Flowers may be pink or white. Rarer in Scotland. June-July. 1-3 m.

▼ Knotgrass
Waste ground, fields and seashores. A low, far-spreading plant. July-October. Creeping stems 3-200 cm.

Great Willowherb ▶
Ditches, marshes, near streams. Rare in northern Scotland. July-August. 80-150 cm.

◀ Sea Bindweed
Sandy beaches; sometimes shingle. Rare in Scotland. June-August. Trailing stems up to 50 cm.

▼ Sand Spurrey
Sandy or gravelly places. Leaves end in a small bristle. May-September. 5-25 cm.

▲ Sea Milkwort
Grassy saltmarshes. Creeping stems. June-August. 10-30 cm tall.

◀ Thrift
Rocky cliffs near coast; mountains inland. March-October. 5-30 cm.

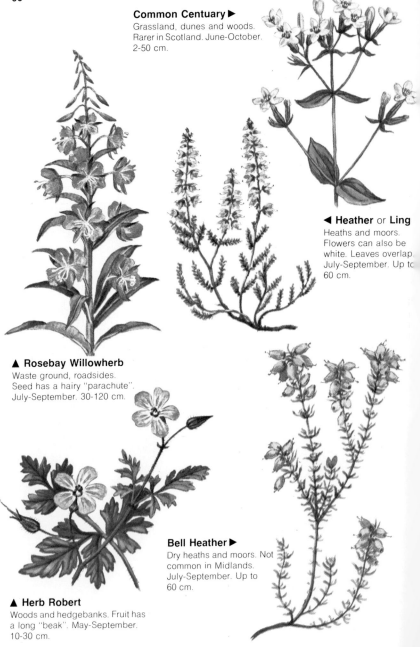

Common Centuary ▶
Grassland, dunes and woods.
Rarer in Scotland. June-October.
2-50 cm.

◀ Heather or **Ling**
Heaths and moors.
Flowers can also be
white. Leaves overlap.
July-September. Up to
60 cm.

▲ Rosebay Willowherb
Waste ground, roadsides.
Seed has a hairy "parachute".
July-September. 30-120 cm.

Bell Heather ▶
Dry heaths and moors. Not
common in Midlands.
July-September. Up to
60 cm.

▲ Herb Robert
Woods and hedgebanks. Fruit has
a long "beak". May-September.
10-30 cm.

▼ Bilberry

Heaths, moors and woods.
Blue-black berries. Flowers
April-June. Up to 60 cm.

Ragged Robin ▲

Damp meadows,
marshes, woods. Sepals
form a tube. May-June.
30-75 cm.

Lady's Smock ▼

Damp meadows and near streams.
Flower can be pink or white and
lilac. April-June. 15-60 cm.

▲ Lesser Knapweed

Grassland and waysides. Stem is
grooved below flowerhead.
June-September. 15-60 cm.

◀ **Hemp Agrimony**

Damp places. Local to rare in Scotland. July-September. 30-120 cm.

▲ **Policeman's Helmet**

River banks, waste places, and near streams. Rare in some areas. July-October. 1-2 m.

Foxglove ▶

Open woods, hedgerows, heaths. Poisonous. June-September. 50-150 cm.

▼ **Valerian**

Scrub, woods and grassy places. June-August. 20-150 cm.

◀ **Red Campion**

Woodlands and hedgerows. Rare in some areas. May-June. 30-90 cm.

◄ Watermint
Near water, marshes,
damp woods.
July-October. 15-90 cm.

**Early Purple
Orchid ►**
Woods and copses.
Locally common
throughout Britain.
May-June. 15-60 cm.

**◄ Devil's Bit
Scabious**
Wet grassy places.
June-October.
15-100 cm.

◄ Wild Teasel
Roadsides, woodland
edges, near streams.
July-August. 50-200 cm.

Field Scabious
y grassland, waste
aces. June-
eptember. 15-80 cm.

**Common Dog
Violet ►**
Hedgerows and
woods.
April-July.
5-20 cm.

Tufted Vetch ▼
Climbs on other plants in hedges
and grassy places. June-August.
Flowers 10 mm long.

▲ Ivy-leaved Toadflax
Old walls, occasionally rocks.
Often forms clumps. May-September.
Flowers 10 mm long.

Sea Lavender ▼
Muddy saltmarshes. Often forms
large mats. Not in northern
Scotland. July-October. 8-30 cm.

▲ Woody Nightshade
Hedges, woods, waste places. Poisonous
Not common in Scotland. June-September
Scrambling stems 30-200 cm.

▼ Long-headed Poppy
Corn and other fields and waste ground.
Longer capsule and paler petals than
Field Poppy. June-July. 20-60 cm.

Capsule

▲ Scarlet Pimpernel
Cultivated and waste ground. A
sub-species has small blue flowers.
Rarer in Scotland. June-August.
6-30 cm.

Capsule

◄ Field Poppy
Corn and other fields,
waste ground. Rare in
northern Scotland.
June-August. 20-60 cm.

▼ Wood Woundwort
Woods, hedgebanks,
waste ground.
July-August.
30-100 cm.

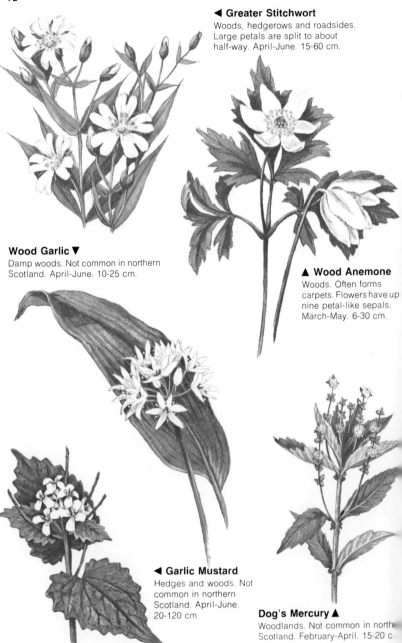

◀ Greater Stitchwort
Woods, hedgerows and roadsides. Large petals are split to about half-way. April-June. 15-60 cm.

Wood Garlic ▼
Damp woods. Not common in northern Scotland. April-June. 10-25 cm.

▲ Wood Anemone
Woods. Often forms carpets. Flowers have up nine petal-like sepals. March-May. 6-30 cm.

◀ Garlic Mustard
Hedges and woods. Not common in northern Scotland. April-June. 20-120 cm.

Dog's Mercury ▲
Woodlands. Not common in north Scotland. February-April. 15-20 c

▼ White Bryony
Climbs in hedges and scrub. Berries are poisonous. Rarer in Scotland. May-September. Up to 4 m.

▼ Wild Strawberry
Woods and scrubland. Leaves have three leaflets. Can cover large patches. April-July.

Cow Parsley ▼
Hedgebanks, roadsides, ditches. Leaves are divided into feathery segments. April-June. 60-100 cm.

▼ Upright Hedge Parsley
Roadsides, grassy places. Flowers later than Cow Parsley, and leaves less feathery. July-August. 50-125 cm.

74

▼ Meadowsweet
Marshes, water meadows and near ditches. Flowers smell sweet. May-September 60-120 cm.

▲ Water Crowfoot
Ponds, streams and ditches. May-June. Flowers are 10-20 mm across.

Wild Carrot ▶
Grassy places, especially near the sea. June-August. 30-100 cm.

Hogweed ▲
Open woods, roadsides, grassy places. June-September. 50-200 cm.

Daisy ▲
Short grassland, especially lawns. March-October. 3-12 cm.

▲ Nettle
Waysides, waste ground, woods. Has stinging hairs. June-August. 30-150 cm.

▼ White Dead Nettle
Roadsides, hedgerows and waste ground. Rare in north Scotland. May-December. 20-60 cm.

▼ White Clover
Garden lawns, grassy places. June-September. Upright stems up to 25 cm.

▲ Shepherd's Purse
Waysides and waste ground. Flowers all year. 3-40 cm.

◀ White Campion
Waysides, hedgebanks, waste
ground. Sticky hairs. May-September.
30-100 cm.

**◀ Bladder
Campion**
Roadsides and grassy
places. Usually
hairless. June-August.
25-90 cm.

◀ Sea Campion
Sea cliffs, shingle beaches.
Smaller than Bladder Campion
with broader petals.
June-August. 8-25 cm.

▼ Chickweed
Fields, waste places,
gardens. Flowers all year.
5-40 cm.

▲ Corn Spurrey
Cornfields, cultivate
land. June-August.
7-40 cm.

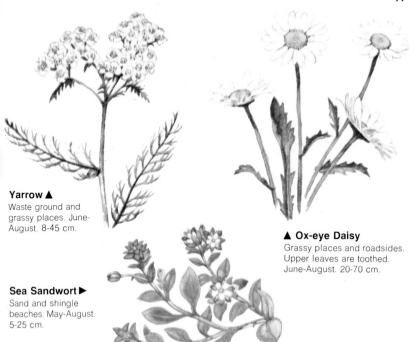

Yarrow ▲
Waste ground and
grassy places. June-
August. 8-45 cm.

Sea Sandwort ▶
Sand and shingle
beaches. May-August.
5-25 cm.

▲ Ox-eye Daisy
Grassy places and roadsides.
Upper leaves are toothed.
June-August. 20-70 cm.

▼ Pellitory-of-the-wall
Wall and rock crevices. Not in
northern Scotland. June-October.
30-100 cm.

▲ Wood Sorrel
Woods and hedgebanks. Flowers
close at night and in bad weather.
Petals have lilac veins. April-May. 5-15 cm.

Blackberry

▲ Black Nightshade
Cultivated and waste ground. Rare in
Scotland. July-September. Up to 60 cm.

▲ Bramble
Woods, scrubland, hedges, open
ground. May-September. Arching
stems up to 5 m.

▼ Greater Plantain
Cultivated land, waysides,
lawns. Broad leaves.
May-September. 10-15 cm.

▲ Ribwort Plantain
Grassy and waste places, lawns.
Ribbed leaves. April-August.
Up to 45 cm.

Butterflies

▲ Wall Brown
Woodlands and rough, open ground. Often rests on walls. Not in northern Scotland. Seen March-September. 44-46 mm.

Wall Brown ♂

▲ Grayling
Sandy places, chalk downs. Less common in Wales and East Anglia. Seen July-August. 56-61 mm.

Grayling ♀

Meadow Brown ♀

▲ Meadow Brown
Meadows and other grassy places. Less common in Scotland. Seen June-September 50-55 mm.

Small Heath ▶
Many areas including open woods, marshes and dry hillsides. Seen April-September. 33-35 mm.

Painted Lady ▶
Dry, open places. Likes thistles. Seen June-October. 62-65 mm.

Painted Lady

Red Admiral ▶
Gardens and woodland edges. Migrant from North Africa. Seen May-October. 66-68 mm.

▲ Small Tortoiseshell
Gardens and open places. Less widespread in Wales and Scotland. Seen April-November. 48-52 mm.
▼

Small Tortoiseshell

▲ Peacock
Gardens. Not present in northern Scotland. Seen August-October. 62-68 mm.

▲ Orange Tip
Woodland edges and hedgerows. Not in parts of Scotland. Seen April-June. 42-48 mm.

♀

♂

Orange Tip

▲ Common Blue
Prefers downs and rough meadows. Seen April-September. 28-36 mm.

♀

♂

Common Blue

♂

▼ Small Copper
All types of country. Less widespread in Scotland. Seen May-September. 26-30 mm.

Caterpillar of Small Copper

♂

♀

♂

▲ Large White
Woods, gardens and open places. Caterpillar eats brassicas. Seen May-August. 62-64 mm.

♂

♀

Large White ♀

♀

Brimstone ♂

▲ Brimstone
Hedges, gardens and woodland paths.
Adult hibernates. Not in Scotland. Seen
June-September. 58-60 mm.

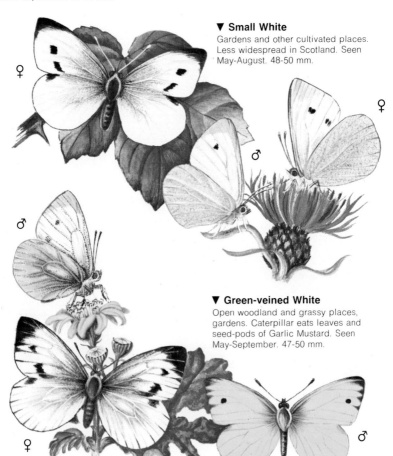

▼ Small White
Gardens and other cultivated places.
Less widespread in Scotland. Seen
May-August. 48-50 mm.

▼ Green-veined White
Open woodland and grassy places,
gardens. Caterpillar eats leaves and
seed-pods of Garlic Mustard. Seen
May-September. 47-50 mm.

Seashore

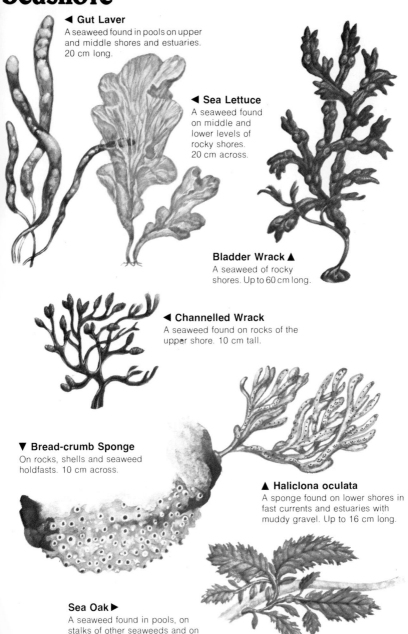

◀ Gut Laver
A seaweed found in pools on upper and middle shores and estuaries. 20 cm long.

◀ Sea Lettuce
A seaweed found on middle and lower levels of rocky shores. 20 cm across.

Bladder Wrack ▲
A seaweed of rocky shores. Up to 60 cm long.

◀ Channelled Wrack
A seaweed found on rocks of the upper shore. 10 cm tall.

▼ Bread-crumb Sponge
On rocks, shells and seaweed holdfasts. 10 cm across.

▲ Haliclona oculata
A sponge found on lower shores in fast currents and estuaries with muddy gravel. Up to 16 cm long.

Sea Oak ▶
A seaweed found in pools, on stalks of other seaweeds and on rocks. 20 cm tall.

▼ Beadlet Anemone
Rock pools at most levels of the shore. 5 cm high.

▼ Snakelocks Anemone
Rocky shores. Not on east or south-east coasts. Can be grey or greenish. 10 cm across.

▲ Daisy Anemone
In rock crevices or mud of shallow pools. 10 cm high.

Dahlia Anemone

▲ Dahlia Anemone
In crevices in rock pools. 15 cm high when open.

◀ Hermit Crab Anemone
On mollusc shells inhabited by Hermit Crab. 10 cm high.

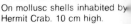

◀ Common Hermit Crab
Mostly lower shore, in rock pools. 5-10 cm long.

▲ Common Limpet
On rocky shores, attached to rocks. 7 cm long.

▲ Common Periwinkle
On rocky and muddy shores. 2.5 cm high.

▲ Netted Dog Whelk
On mud and gravel off shore and on lower shore. 2.5 cm high.

▲ Saddle Oyster
On lower shore, attached to rocks. 6 cm wide.

▲ Common Whelk
Lower shore of rocky or sandy beaches. 8 cm high.

▲ Slipper Limpet
Low water and off shore, often attached to one another. 4-5 cm long.

▲ Common Mussel
Rocky shores, pier piles and estuaries. 1-10 cm long.

▲ Dog Whelk
On rocks and in crevices of lower shore. 3 cm high.

▲ Painted Topshell
On rocks and under stones on lower shore. 2.5 cm high.

▲ Common Oyster
Shallow and deep water. 10-15 cm long.

▲ **Necklace Shell**
Sandy shores. 3 cm high.

▲ **Rayed Trough Shell**
Sand or gravel on lower shores. 5 cm long.

▲ **Razor Shell**
Burrows in mud. 12 cm long.

▲ **Baltic Tellin**
In mud and sand of seashores and estuaries.
2 cm long.

▲ **Common Sand Gaper**
Burrows in muddy sand on lower shore.
12 cm wide.

▲ **Horse Mussel**
From lower shore to deep water. 20 cm long

▲ **Edible Cockle**
In mud and sand of middle shore and below.
4 cm across.

▲ **Flat Periwinkle**
Under brown seaweed on rocky shores.
1 cm high.

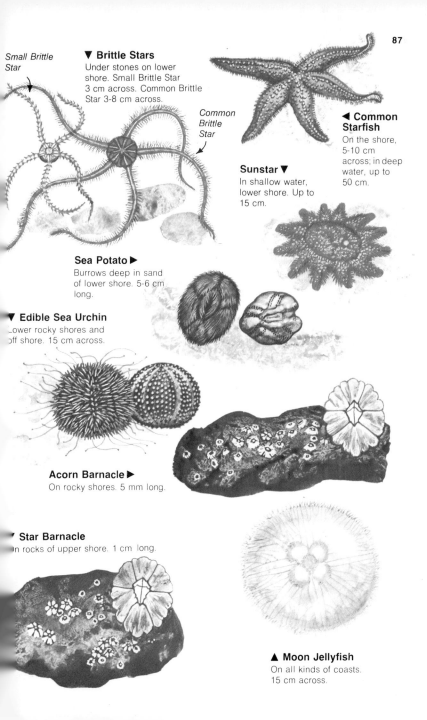

Small Brittle Star

▼ Brittle Stars
Under stones on lower shore. Small Brittle Star 3 cm across. Common Brittle Star 3-8 cm across.

Common Brittle Star

◄ Common Starfish
On the shore, 5-10 cm across; in deep water, up to 50 cm.

Sunstar ▼
In shallow water, lower shore. Up to 15 cm.

Sea Potato ►
Burrows deep in sand of lower shore. 5-6 cm long.

▼ Edible Sea Urchin
Lower rocky shores and off shore. 15 cm across.

Acorn Barnacle ►
On rocky shores. 5 mm long.

▼ Star Barnacle
On rocks of upper shore. 1 cm long.

▲ Moon Jellyfish
On all kinds of coasts. 15 cm across.

▲ Common Prawn
Shallow water and rock pools. 5-8 cm long.

▲ White Shrimp
Rock pools on lower shore; shallow waters of estuaries. 5 cm long.

▲ Sand Shrimp
Sand estuaries. 5 cm long.

▲ Shore Crab
Sandy, muddy and rocky shores; estuaries. 8 cm across.

▲ Broad-clawed Porcelain Crab
Under stones on middle and lower shores. 1.2 cm across.

▼ Common Lobster
Only small ones in rock pools of lower shore. Can grow up to 45 cm long elsewhere.

▼ Montagu's Plated Lobster
Under seaweed and stones of lower shore. 4-6 cm long.

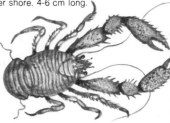

▼ Edible Crab
Only small ones in rock pools in lower shore. Can grow up to 11.5 cm long elsewhere.

Cuttlebone

▲ Common Cuttlefi
In sheltered bays and washed up dead on strand line. 30 cm long.

Trees

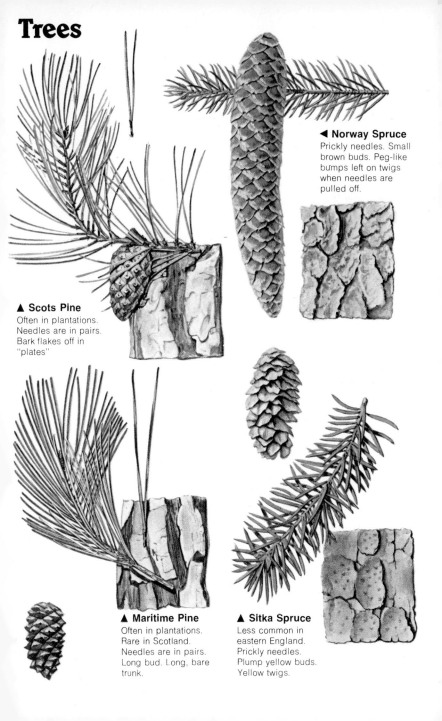

◄ Norway Spruce
Prickly needles. Small brown buds. Peg-like bumps left on twigs when needles are pulled off.

▲ Scots Pine
Often in plantations. Needles are in pairs. Bark flakes off in "plates"

▲ Maritime Pine
Often in plantations. Rare in Scotland. Needles are in pairs. Long bud. Long, bare trunk.

▲ Sitka Spruce
Less common in eastern England. Prickly needles. Plump yellow buds. Yellow twigs.

▼ European Larch
Deciduous. Bunches of soft, light green needles leave small knobs on twigs when they fall.

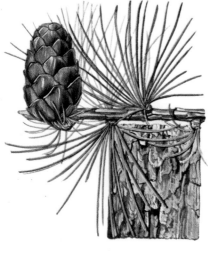

▲ Douglas Fir
Soft, fragrant needles. Cones have three-pointed bracts on each scale.

▼ European Silver Fir
Rare in east and south-east England. Needles are green above, silvery below.

▲ Corsican Pine
Often in plantations. Needles are in pairs. Onion-shaped buds.

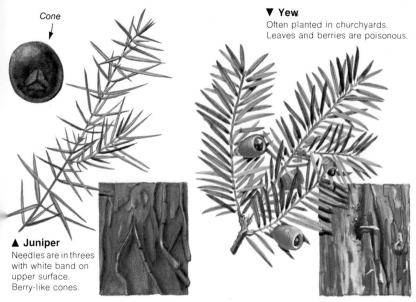

Cone

▼ Yew
Often planted in churchyards.
Leaves and berries are poisonous.

▲ Juniper
Needles are in threes
with white band on
upper surface.
Berry-like cones.

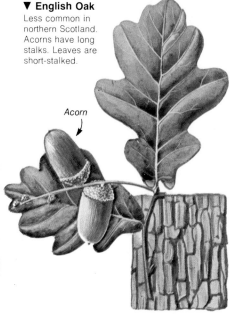

▼ English Oak
Less common in
northern Scotland.
Acorns have long
stalks. Leaves are
short-stalked.

Acorn

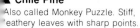

▲ Chile Pine
Also called Monkey Puzzle. Stiff,
leathery leaves with sharp points.

▼ Common Ash
Less common in northern Scotland. Seeds are in clusters called "keys".

Seeds

Flowers

▼ Rowan
Clusters of flowers appear in May. Berries ripen in August.

Rowan flower

▲ Common Alder
Always found near water. Reddish catkins ripen to cone-like fruits.

Fruit

▲ Sessile Oak
Acorn is usually stalkless. Leaves are long-stalked.

Acorn

▼ Aspen
Often grows in thickets. Leaves tremble in the wind. White downy catkins appear in May on female trees.

Catkin

▲ Goat Willow
Common on damp waste ground and in scrub woodland. Catkins, known as "Pussy Willows", appear in late winter.

▼ White Willow
Common by water. Not in north-west Scotland. Weeping Willow is a variety of this species.

Catkin

Catkin

▲ Silver Birch
Catkins, known as "lamb's tails", are yellow with pollen in April. Bark peels off in ribbons.

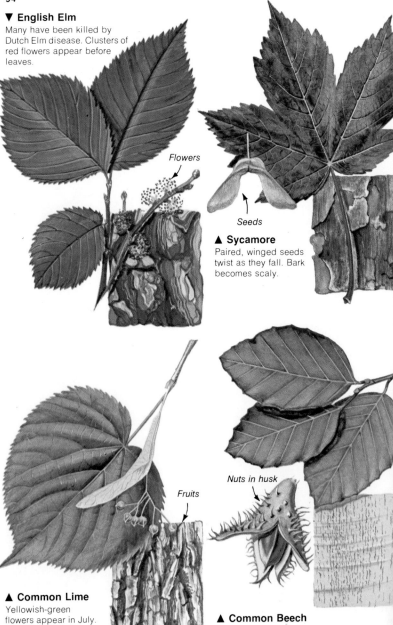

▼ English Elm
Many have been killed by Dutch Elm disease. Clusters of red flowers appear before leaves.

Flowers

Seeds

▲ Sycamore
Paired, winged seeds twist as they fall. Bark becomes scaly.

Fruits

▲ Common Lime
Yellowish-green flowers appear in July. Fruits hang from leafy wing.

Nuts in husk

▲ Common Beech
Leaves turn copper-brown in autumn. Nuts are triangular, encased in a husk.

▼ Sweet Chestnut
Flowers appear in
June. Edible chestnuts
are encased in a
prickly fruit.

Flowers

Fruits

▲ Horse Chestnut
Less common in Scotland. "Candles" of
flowers (white or pink) appear in May.

Holly
Less common in northern
Scotland. Evergreen. Berries
found only on female trees.

Flowers

**▲ Common
Hawthorn**
Grows in thickets and
hedgerows. Berries
usually have only one
stone.

The leaves and bark of each of the species shown below are illustrated on page 89–95.

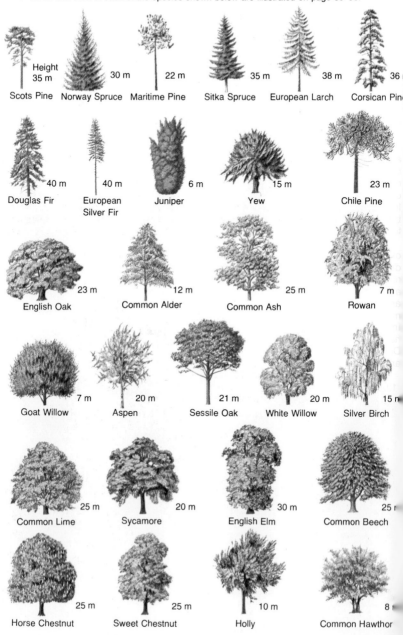

Height
35 m
Scots Pine

30 m
Norway Spruce

22 m
Maritime Pine

35 m
Sitka Spruce

38 m
European Larch

36 m
Corsican Pine

40 m
Douglas Fir

40 m
European
Silver Fir

6 m
Juniper

15 m
Yew

23 m
Chile Pine

23 m
English Oak

12 m
Common Alder

25 m
Common Ash

7 m
Rowan

7 m
Goat Willow

20 m
Aspen

21 m
Sessile Oak

20 m
White Willow

15 m
Silver Birch

25 m
Common Lime

20 m
Sycamore

30 m
English Elm

25 m
Common Beech

25 m
Horse Chestnut

25 m
Sweet Chestnut

10 m
Holly

8 m
Common Hawthorn

Places to Visit

This section describes a large selection of places to visit, many of which are good examples of the habitats described at the beginning of the book. The places listed range from nature reserves, country parks and good birdwatching areas to zoos, gardens and museums. Many reserves, country parks and forests have marked nature trails with accompanying leaflets, designed to inform the visitor of the wildlife of the area. Where a site has a trail, this information is included in the description.

The descriptions of the places to visit are grouped by county in alphabetical order. Each place is marked by a number on a map which appears at the beginning of the section for each county. Notable long distance footpaths are also marked, but not numbered; their descriptions are found immediately below the maps.

The descriptions outline the main points of interest in each place. They also give details about location and approach by road. Where relevant, telephone numbers and general restrictions on opening times are also included. To avoid disappointment, the visitor is advised to check these in advance, as in some cases opening hours are irregular and liable to change. Details of opening times for Bank Holidays and the Christmas period are not given.

In most cases, the Ordnance Survey (1:50 000) map number and grid reference is given, at the very end of the description (eg. OS 142: 205 890). The sheet number follows after "OS" and the grid reference after the colon. For large areas such as forests, the reference given is often for a car park or a point of access, such as the beginning of a footpath.

It is not possible to list every site of interest, but further information can be obtained locally and by consulting the relevant Ordnance Survey map. The English Tourist Board publishes a range of literature on the region, and this can be obtained from the Regional Tourist Board Offices (see page 123). Tourist Information Centres are run in many areas, particularly during the summer months, and these provide both literature and details of current opening times for local places of interest. Other useful addresses for organisations such as the National Trust are also given on page 123.

East Sussex

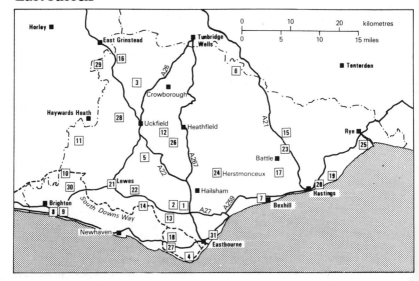

South Downs Way

Long distance bridleway and footpath in West and East Sussex along the South Downs from Eastbourne to the Hampshire border. Open to horseriders, cyclists and walkers along most of the route (the alternative coastal path between Eastbourne and Alfriston is for walkers only). Fine views; good selection of birds, butterflies and flowers. Areas of particular interest in East Sussex are described in the list of places to visit below. The route is well signposted; walkers and others are advised to keep to official paths and to avoid crossing private land.

☐ The Countryside Commission publish a leaflet describing the route and have made available an official guidebook: *South Downs Way*, by Seán Jennett, published by Her Majesty's Stationery Office. The leaflet is available from the Countryside Commission, John Dower House, Crescent Place, Cheltenham, Glos GL50 3RA (Tel: Cheltenham 21381). OS sheets 197, 198, 199.

1 Abbots Wood

Forestry Commission. Ancient deciduous woodland with a pond where waterbirds may be seen. Forest trail.

☐ 7 miles/11 km north of Eastbourne along A22; take turning east to Arlington. OS 199: 557 075.

2 Arlington Reservoir

Local Nature Reserve. Good for wildfowl especially during autumn migration; in winter Wigeon, Tufted Duck and Shoveler together with large numbers of Canada Geese, are present.

☐ Access only along footpath around the reservoir. North-east of Eastbourne along A27; take road to Berwick. Reservoir is just north of Berwick station. OS 199: 525 075.

3 Ashdown Forest

Area of open heathland and woodland at western end of the High Weald. About 6400 acres/2590 ha are open to the public, the rest is mainly enclosed farmland. Good for flora and fauna. For a detailed description see Garth Christian's *Ashdown Forest*, available from the Society of Friends of Ashdown Forest, The Square, Forest Row.

☐ West of Crowborough. Access off B2188 at Camp Hill onto unclassified road (OS 188: 460 287) or off B2026 near Gills Lap (OS 188: 467 317). Visitors are reminded to guard against fire.

4 Beachy Head

Chalk cliffs with magnificent views. Good area for migrant birds, especially the smaller ones, in spring and autumn; migrant butterflies in summer. Nature trail and Natural History Centre prepared by the Eastbourne Natural History and Archaeological Society, near the Coastguard Station. Leaflet available for trail on site, or from Seven Sisters Country Park Centre (see 27).

☐The most southerly part of East Sussex, on road between Eastbourne and Eastdean. Centre open Easter–September, Saturday and Sunday afternoons. OS 199: 565 975.

5 Bentley Wildfowl Reserve

Excellent collection of waterfowl in a delightful setting.

☐Bentley, Halland, Lewes (Tel: Halland 573). Open daily, Easter–September; weekends only in winter. Closed in December. 7 miles/11 km north-east of Lewes, on B2129. OS 198: 485 160

6 Bewl Bridge Reservoir

The largest reservoir south of the Thames; good for freshwater birds; access limited but good views from the bank in places.

☐Reservoir lies south-east of Tunbridge Wells. Information Centre open daily. Signposted off A21, 1 mile/1.6 km south of Lamberhurst. OS 188: 686 337.

7 Bexhill Museum

Local natural history and geology exhibits; local history.

☐Egerton Road (Tel: Bexhill 211769). Open weekdays except Friday

8 Booth Museum of Natural History

A fine collection of British birds exceptionally well displayed; butterfly collection; interesting exhibit of evolution and adaption of animals' skeletons.

☐194 Dyke Road, Brighton (Tel: Brighton 552586). Open daily except Thursday.

9 Brighton Aquarium and Dolphinarium

Collection of fish and marine animals including dolphins, sea-lions, turtles and terrapins.

☐Marine Parade, Brighton (Tel: Brighton 604233). Open daily, all year. Near Palace Pier on A259.

10 Ditchling Beacon

Sussex Trust for Nature conservation reserve adjoining National Trust Property. Situated on the north-facing scarp slope of the South Downs; excellent views when clear. Chalk grassland and scrub with many typical flowers; clumps of Hemp Agrimony along the crest attract many insects including Blue butterflies.

☐On South Downs Way. 1½ miles/3 km south of Ditchling (5 miles/8 km north of Brighton). OS 198: 328 133.

11 Ditchling Common Country Park

An old Weald clay common with developing woodland; nature trail. Good selection of birds, flowers, and butterflies. Trail leaflet available at the start. Ranger usually on site or may be reached at Seven Sisters Country Park (Tel: Alfriston 870250).

☐Just east of Burgess Hill at intersection of B2113 and B2112. OS 198: 335 180.

12 Dower House Farm Trail

Interesting dairy farm; emphasis on countryside conservation. Trail leaflet.

☐(Tel: Heathfield 2016). Trail on open all year. Near Blackboys, 2½ miles/4 km west of Heathfield. Access of B2102 at Sharlands. OS 199: 533 201.

13 Drusillas Zoo

Small but interesting collection. Mainly small animals; tropical birds; aquarium.

☐Alfriston (Tel: Alfriston 870234). Open daily, all year. 4 miles/6 km north-east of Seaford on B2108 just south of intersection with A27. OS 199: 526 048.

14 Firle Beacon

Area of downland with fine views of Glynde Valley; typical downland plants; ancient burial mounds.

☐On South Downs Way. 4 miles/6 km north-east of Newhaven. Access to Beacon by footpath only; top of scarp can be reached by road leading off A27 near Preston House. OS 198: 486 060.

15 Footland Wood
Forestry Commission. Pine and Beech-woods. Forest trail from picnic place; leaflets available.
☐8 miles/13 km north of Hastings along A21; turn east along B2089. OS 199: 763 203.

16 Forest Way Country Park
Park and nature trail created along a disused railway line. Leaflet available from Council offices, County Planning Dept., Southover House, Southover Road, Lewes.
☐1.8 miles/3 km south-east of East Grinstead on A22. OS 187: 418 357.

17 Fore Wood
RSPB reserve. Deciduous woodland with typical birds, butterflies and flowers.
☐Access along marked footpaths. 3 miles/ 4.8 km north of Bexhill at Crowhurst. OS 199: 755 130.

18 Friston Forest
Forestry Commission. Young Beech and Pinewoods. Forest trail from picnic place; leaflet available at start, or from Seven Sisters Country Park (see 27).
☐West of Eastbourne along A259; turn north at Exceat, beyond East Dean. OS 199: 518 002.

19 Hastings Country Park
540 acres/219 ha of land with wooded glens situated along a five-mile stretch of coast. Access to beach at Fairlight Glen. Six nature trails with leaflets available from the Interpretive Centre in the park, or from the Tourism and Recreation Information Centre in Hastings.
☐East of Hastings; take road to Fairlight off A259. Park open at all times; Interpretive centre at parking place near Fairlight, open weekends during the summer. Tourism Centre, 4 Robertson Terrace, Hastings (Tel: Hastings 424242). Open daily in summer; closed Saturday afternoons and Sundays in winter.

20 Hastings Museum and Art Gallery
Natural history exhibits; prehistoric animals and archaeology.
☐St John's Place, Cambridge Road, Hastings (Tel: Hastings 435952). Open daily; afternoons only on Sundays.

21 Lewes Museum of Sussex Archaeology
Excellent for archaeology and appreciation of man's gradual impact on the environment.
☐Barbican House, High Street, Lewes (Tel: Lewes 4379). Open Monday–Saturday throughout the year; also Sunday afternoons from April–October.

22 Mount Caburn
Area of open downland with typical flowers and butterflies. Iron Age fort; fine views, with line of North Downs and Box Hill visible when clear.
☐2 miles/3 km south-east of Lewes. Access by path from Glynde. OS 198: 445 090.

23 Norton's Farm Museum
A fruit and arable farm typical of the South-East; collection of old farm implements; farm trail.
☐Kent Street, Sedlescombe (Tel: Sedlescombe 471). Open daily mid-June–September. OS 199: 784 156.

24 Royal Greenwich Observatory Exhibition
Astronomy and history of Observatory; the Sussex Trust for Nature Conservation have a section of natural history exhibits; formal gardens.
☐(Tel: Herstmonceux 3171). Open Easter–September, afternoons daily mornings also at weekends. At Herstmonceux, off A271.

25 Rye Harbour
Shingle beach and old flooded gravel workings; damp meadows and ditches inland. Part of the area is a local nature reserve with two hides open to the public. Information Centre in harbour cark park Typical shingle plants including Sea Pea Very good area for birds. Many gulls ducks and waders at all times of the year At migration times, Avocet, Black an Sandwich Tern, finches and warblers ca be seen. In winter look out for Bar-taile

and Black-tailed Godwits, Common Scoter, Curlew, Dunlin, Eider Duck, Gadwall, Pintail and Velvet Scoter (offshore). ☐Information Centre open April–September, daily; October–March, Saturday, Sunday and Wednesday afternoons. Access from Rye Harbour, south-east of Rye; also by public footpath from Winchelsea Beach. Please keep to footpaths. OS 189: 930 180.

☐**Pett Level**. Freshwater pools nearby are also good for birds. View from road which runs from Winchelsea Beach to Cliff End. OS 189: 903 148.

☐**Northpoint Beach**. Gravel workings; waders and ducks. East of Rye; views from East Guldeford to Camber road. OS 189: 935 200.

26 Selwyns Wood

Nature reserve. Sussex Trust for Nature Conservation. Mixed deciduous woodland with good example of Sweet Chestnut coppice. Woodland plants and birds. Please keep to paths.

☐West of Heathfield on Waldron to Cross-in-Hand road. Access from Firgrove Road, Rosers Cross. OS 199: 552 204.

27 Seven Sisters Country Park

Interesting sunken estuary on the South Downs; access to the seashore at Cuckmere Haven. Nature trail and Country Park Centre; typical chalkland plants, saltmarsh and maritime flowers. Leaflets and other publications available from the Centre which also has good displays of natural history and development of the area.

☐(Tel: Alfriston 870250). Centre open daily, Good Friday–October; weekends only in winter. East of Seaford on A259 by Exceat Bridge. OS 199: 525 986.

☐**Seaford Head Nature Reserve**, on west side of River Cuckmere, is also worth visiting. Guide leaflets available from Seven Sisters Country Park OS 199: 510 975.

28 Sheffield Park Garden

National Trust. Woodlands and park originally by Capability Brown. Extensively planted in this century with many unusual shrubs; several lakes. On one side of car park is a bird sanctuary where sick and injured birds are cared for.

☐(Tel: Danehill 790655). Open 1st April–14 November, Tuesday–Saturday; afternoons only on Sundays. On east side of A275, 3 miles/5 km north of Chailey. OS 198: 409 242.

29 Springhill Wildfowl Park

Set in beautiful grounds on borders of Ashdown Forest. Fine collection of birds including peacocks, flamingos, cranes, and rare geese.

☐(Tel: Forest Row 2783). Open daily, all year. Near East Grinstead, 1 mile/1.5 km south-west of Forest Row. OS 187: 405 345.

30 Stanmer Park

Interesting piece of chalk downland with typical flowers and butterflies; nature trail. Leaflet available from Stanmer Village Post Office.

☐Open daily, all year. North-eastern edge of Brighton, off A27. OS 198: 340 097.

31 Towner Art Gallery

Collection of British butterflies and moths; paintings, including some Sussex landscapes.

☐9 Borough Lane, Eastbourne (Tel: Eastbourne 21635). Open daily; afternoons only on Sundays.

Hampshire

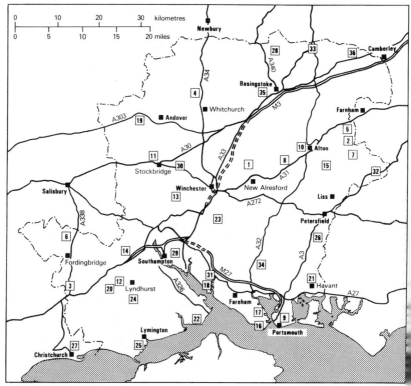

1 Abbotstone Down
☐Interesting area of mixed woodland and open downland. The ground is not pure chalk as can be seen by the patches of dark reddish soil and the presence of Oak trees. Ash and a few Yews also grow here. Shrubs include Buckthorn, Dogwood, Spindle, Wayfaring Tree and Wild Privet; also some old coppiced Hazels. Turtle Dove, Bullfinch and Linnet in scrub. Characteristic flowers and butterflies on the open downland areas.
☐2 miles/3 km north of New Alresford on B3046. OS 185: 583 362.

2 Alice Holt Forest
Forestry Commission. Superb area of deciduous and coniferous woods; fine trees. Typical birds, plants and butterflies. Forest walks; leaflets available from the Information Centre.

☐(Tel: Bentley 3135). Centre open weekdays. 5 miles/8 km south of Farnham (Surrey) along A325; for Information Centre, take road eastwards at Bucks Horn Oak. OS 186: 810 412.

3 Avon Valley
Mostly private land but there are good views from roads (especially Ibsley to Harbridge road) and beside old gravel pits. Look out for Kingfisher, Grey and Pied Wagtails, Little Grebe and Mute Swan. In winter Tufted Duck, Wigeon, White-fronted Goose may be seen in the old gravel pits; various waders in the valley.
☐North of Ringwood along both sides of A338. OS 195: 150 070.

4 Beacon Hill
Old hill fort with fine views from the top. Hawthorn and Buckthorn scrub below

Good area for chalkland flowers. Rather wind-swept for butterflies but Blues and Skippers do occur.
☐5 miles/8 km north of Whitchurch, west off A34. OS 174: 458 573.

5 Birdworld Zoological Gardens

Good collection of waterfowl, birds of prey, pheasants, penguins and hardier tropical birds.
☐Holt Pound, near Farnham, Surrey (Tel: Bentley 2140). Open daily, all year. 3 miles/5 km south-west of Farnham on A325 Petersfield road. OS 186: 810 440.

6 Breamore House Countryside Museum

Comprehensive displays relating to agriculture.
☐(Tel: Breamore 468). Open April–September, afternoons daily except Monday and Friday; mornings also at weekend. 3 miles/5 km north of Fordingbridge, off the A338.

7 Broxhead Common

Heathland with developing woodland; Oak, Birch, heathers and Gorse. Typical birds.
☐East of Alton along B3004, just south of Sleaford. OS 186: 804 374.

8 Chawton Park Woods

Forestry Commission. Mixed conifer and broadleaved wood. Trail starting from picnic place.
☐4 miles/6.5 km south-west of Alton along A31; turn north at Four Marks. OS 186: 572 362.

9 Cumberland House Museum and Aquarium

Natural history and geology of the Hampshire Basin.
☐Eastern Parade, Southsea, Portsmouth (Tel: Portsmouth 732654). Open daily, all year.

10 The Curtis Museum

Many exhibits including collections of local geology, botany and zoology.
☐High Street, Alton (Tel: Alton 82802). Open daily, except Sunday.

11 Danebury Hill

Iron Age hill fort with good views of surrounding countryside; typical chalkland flowers. A few Juniper bushes and Beech trees. Meadow Pipit, Tree Pipit and Skylark. Trail leaflet available on site.
☐North-west of Stockbridge. Access off A30 at Meon Hill onto unclassified road. OS 185: 324 376.

12 Deer Sanctuary

Forestry Commission. Area in the New Forest with observation hide for viewing deer.
☐Access at all times. 4 miles/6 km west of Lyndhurst on unclassified road through Emery Down. OS 195: 235 085.

13 Farley Mount Country Park

Fine woodlands and open downland. Chalk grassland with typical flowers; woodland birds and downland butterflies.
☐3 miles/5 km west of Winchester. Access from intersection of A3090 and B3041, onto unclassified road. OS 185: 430 293.

14 Furzey Gardens

Good collection of flowering shrubs and other plants; sixteenth-century cottage.
☐(Tel: Cadnam 2464). Open daily, all year. Minstead, on northern side of the New Forest. OS 195: 273 114.

15 Gilbert White Museum and Oates Memorial Library and Museum

Housed in the home of the famous eighteenth-century naturalist, Gilbert White. The White Museum includes an interpretive exhibition of the natural history of Selborne. The Oates Museum has a collection of Antarctic and tropical birds as well as objects relating to the travels of Lawrence Oates in Antarctica, and Frank Oates in Africa. At the back of the museum is a delightful view of Selborne Hanger, a National Trust property with fine Beechwoods, and typical chalkland flowers and birds. Access to this is via the zigzag path behind the Selborne Arms.
☐(Tel: Selborne 275). Open March–October, daily in afternoon except Monday. In Selborne village, 4 miles/ 6 km south of Alton.

16 Gilkicker Point

Area on west side of entrance to Portsmouth Harbour. Good for migrant birds, especially finches, larks, warblers. Eider Duck, Mergansers, Skuas and Divers can be seen offshore in winter.

☐Off B3333 at Gosport. Access to shore at various points near and through golf course. OS 196: 605 975.

17 Gosport Museum

Displays of local natural history and geology; freshwater and marine aquaria.

☐Walpole Road, Gosport (Tel: Gosport 88035). Open Tuesday–Saturday.

18 Hamble Common

Area of marshland overlooking Southampton Water and the Hamble river. Good for birds in winter.

☐South-west of Southampton along A3025; take B3397 to Hamble; Common is just south of Hamble. OS 196:480 060.

19 The Hawk Conservancy

Mainly birds of prey; flown daily during the summer.

☐Sarson Lane, Weyhill (Tel: Weyhill 2252). Open daily March–October. 3 miles/5 km west of Andover, turning off the A303 at Fyfield. OS 185: 308 455.

20 Holiday Hill Reptillary

Collection of reptiles found in the New Forest including Smooth Snake, Common and Sand Lizards.

☐Holiday Hill Cottage, Lyndhurst (Tel: Cadnam 3494). Open daily in summer but opening and closing dates vary according to the weather; best to check beforehand. 2 miles/3 km west of Lyndhurst. Access through Holiday Hill camp site. OS 195: 271 071.

21 Leigh Park Gardens and Farm Trail

Beautiful park and lake; rare breeds of British cattle and other domestic animals.

☐Leigh Park, Havant (Tel: Havant 483759). Open daily Easter–September. 2 miles/ 3 km north of Havant town centre.

22 Lepe Country Park

Interesting coastal area with some maritime vegetation; occasional sea birds offshore. Good views of the Isle of Wight.

☐At Stone Point. Access off A326 onto unclassified road via Blackfield. OS 196: 460 985.

23 Marwell Zoological Park

Excellent country zoo, famous for breeding endangered animals. Deer, big cats (Siberian Tiger), antelopes, rare species of horses, flightless birds.

☐(Tel: Owslebury 206). Open daily, all year. Colden Common, 7 miles/11 km south of Winchester off A333. OS 185: 504 214.

24 New Forest

Mainly Forestry Commission land. 100 square miles/256 square km of deciduous and coniferous woods interspersed with patches of heathland. For description of wildlife see page 29. Many parking and picnic places; several forest walks with leaflets available. Colin Tubbs' book *The New Forest, an Ecological History* (David & Charles) provides an excellent account of the area. (see also 12 and 20).

☐South-west of Southampton along A35. Trail leaflets, guides and maps of the New Forest are available at the Information Centre in the car park at Lyndhurst (Tel: Lyndhurst 2269), open daily Easter–September. At other times of the year these publications are available from the Forestry Commission offices in Southampton Road (Tel: Lyndhurst 2801), open Monday–Friday, or from Margerons Newsagents in the High Street.

25 Pennington Marshes

Interesting saltings and lagoons; good for waders. Green Sandpiper, Greenshank, Little Stint, Ruff and Wood Sandpiper may be seen in spring and autumn. Fine views of Hurst Castle and the Isle of Wight.

☐South of Lymington. Access off A337 to Woodside, then by public footpath. OS 196: 320 925.

26 Queen Elizabeth Country Park

Forestry Commission and Hampshire County Council. 540 acres/218 ha of open downland on Butser Hill; typical chalkland

wers and butterflies. 860 acres/349 ha of
ech and coniferous woodland. Informa-
n Centre; three nature trails (leaflets
ailable from Centre); ancient farm
monstration; forest and woodland craft
ea.
Gravel Hill, Horndean (Tel: Horndean
5040). Park Centre open daily April–
tober; November and March daily
cept Monday and Saturday; Dec-
ber–February, Sunday only. Sign-
sted off A3, 4 miles/6 km south of
tersfield. OS 197: 717 185.

Redhouse Museum
cal natural history displays; marine and
shwater aquaria.
Quay Road, Christchurch (Tel: Christ-
urch 482860). Open Tuesday–Sunday.

Silchester Common/Pamber Forest
athland with rich valley bog; typical
getation, insects and birds. Footpaths
ough ancient Oakwood on acid soil.
North of Basingstoke along A340; take
ning north-east to Silchester. OS 175:
6 611.

Southampton Zoo
ood collection of animals; some birds
d a Reptile House.
he Common, Southampton (Tel:
uthampton 556603). Open daily, all
ar. Access from A33.

Stockbridge Down
tional Trust. Area of chalk downland
th Bronze Age barrows and Iron Age
rt. Wide range of downland flowers (best
more open ground at west end) and
rubs including Buckthorn, Dogwood,
elder Rose, Juniper; Dropwort, Fairy
ax, Hairy Rockcress, Hairy Violet and
tches, Hemlock and Rough Chervil at
all car park at east end. Typical down-
d butterflies; look out for Brimstone
terpillars feeding on Buckthorn leaves.
rds include Corn Bunting, Cuckoo, Lin-
t, Tree Pipit, Willow Warbler (summer)
d Yellowhammer; also finches and other
rblers (summer). Brown Hare, Rabbit,
ole and Roe Deer present.
½ miles/12 km south of Andover, 1

mile/1.5 km east of Stockbridge on north
side of A272. OS 185: 379 349.

31 Upper Hamble Country Park
Area of developing woodland with nature
trail. Typical woodland birds.
☐East of Southampton, on west bank of
River Hamble. Access by footpaths, south
from Hedge End. OS 196: 500 110.

32 Waggoners' Wells and Bramshott Common
National Trust. Woodland, heathland and
ponds. Good selection of trees and birds;
typical acid soil vegetation on top of north
side of valley. Nature Trail leaflets
available from Grayshott Post Office.
☐1½ miles/3 km South-west of Hindhead
(Surrey) between Grayshott and A3.
OS 186: 862 345.

33 Wellington Country Park
Pleasant woodlands; Birchen Copse
Nature Trail. Trail leaflet available from the
reception centre.
☐Heckfield (Tel: Heckfield 444). Open
daily, March–October. Off A32 north of
Heckfield. OS 186: 720 623.

34 West Walk, Forest of Bere
Forestry Commission. Conifers and broad-
leaved trees, mainly Beech, Hazel and
Sweet Chestnut; fine Holly trees and a few
Yews. Woodland butterflies and birds.
Trails beginning from picnic places.
☐North of Wickham along A32. Take tur-
ning east towards Soberton Heath for start
of trail through older trees. OS 196:
592 137.

35 Willis Museum and Art Gallery
Local archaeology, natural history and
geology exhibits. Temporary exhibitions
in art gallery.
☐New Street, Basingstoke (Tel: Basingstoke 65902). Open daily except Sunday;
afternoons only on Mondays.

36 Yately Common Country Park
Interesting area of heathland; nature trail
and picnic area.
☐West of Camberley on A30, south-west of
intersection with A327. OS 186: 830 592.

Isle of Wight

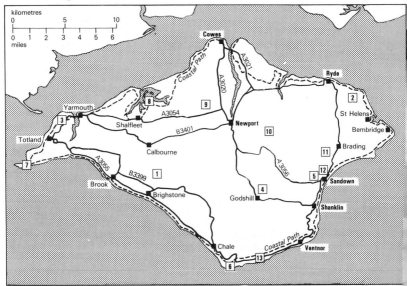

Coastal Path

Long distance footpath around the whole island, mainly close to the sea.

☐Isle of Wight County Council publishes leaflets covering different sections of the path, including information on the wildlife that can be seen. They also publish leaflets on other walks that can be made on the island. These are available from the Tourist Information Centre, 21 High Street, Newport (Tel: Newport 524343) Open Monday–Saturday; mornings only on Saturdays.

Nature Trails

The Isle of Wight Natural History and Archaeological Society have prepared a leaflet to accompany six nature trails on the island. This is available from the Tourist Information Centre (address above). The Society also has an exhibition during August of each year at Seely Hall, Brook.

Brook Nature Trail starting from Seely Hall OS 196: 390 837.

River Medina Nature Trail follows the east bank of the Medina starting from Newport quay. OS 196: 503 896.

Riverside Walk Nature Trail follows the River Yar starting from Alverstone, 2 miles/3.5 kms north-west of Sandown OS 196: 577 857.

Riverside Walk Nature Trail follows the River Yar on the east side of the island Approach river from the car park opposite the ferry entrance at Yarmouth. OS 196 355 894.

Blackgang Nature Trail along part of the south coast, beginning at the car par above Blackgang. OS 196: 490 767.

Carisbrooke Walk Nature Trail beginning from the car park overlooking Carisbrook Castle, south-west of Newport. OS 196 483 866.

1 Brighstone Forest

Forestry Commission. Pine and Beech woods. Forest walk leads through wood to open downland owned by the Nation Trust. Fine views of the south coast ar The Needles.

☐West of Newport along B3401; turn sou at Calbourne; 2½ miles/4 km along th road is parking place where walk begin OS 196: 420 846.

2 Flamingo Park

About 80 different species of waterfo including flamingos, swans and gees

Also peacocks, pheasants and cranes. Pets' Corner. Mostly out-of-doors, overlooking Spithead Waters.
☐Oakhill Road, Spring Vale, Seaview (Tel: Seaview 2153). Open daily, April–September. 2 miles/3 km east of Ryde on B3330. OS 196: 621 918.

3 Fort Victoria Country Park
Nature trail through woodland (Pine and Holm Oak), scrub plants and ferns. Leaflet available from Tourist Information Centre, 21 High Street, Newport (Tel: Newport 524343). Centre open Monday–Saturday; Saturday, mornings only.
☐Just west of Yarmouth along A3054; take road north to coast at Norton. OS 196: 340 898.

4 Godshill Natural History Collection
Marvellous collections of British and tropical butterflies, precious and semi-precious stones, minerals and seashells.
☐High Street, Godshill (Tel: Godshill 333). Open daily, May–September.

5 Isle of Wight Zoo
Collection of endangered animals, including birds; reptiles, and demonstration of "milking" snakes for their venom.
☐Yaverland Fort, Sandown (Tel: Sandown 403883). Open daily, July–September.

Knowles Farm, St Catherine's Point
National Trust. Interesting cliffs, mainly of clay. Good for coastal plants, butterflies and birds.
☐Access by footpaths off A3055. OS 196: 497 754.

The Needles Headland
National Trust. Chalk cliffs and downland ; western end of island; whole area is a bird sanctuary. Fine views of coast; interesting chalkland flowers. Birds include Guillemot, Kittiwake and Puffin. Headon Warren is notable for heathland vegetation.
☐Access from Alum Bay (car park and chair lift) on B3322. Footpaths to Headon Warren, Tennyson Down and to look-out at Scratchell's Bay. OS 196: 330 848.

8 Newtown Marsh
Nature Reserve. Ise of Wight County Council. Saltmarshes where many waders, ducks and geese can be seen in autumn and winter. Nature trail; leaflet available from National Trust office in Newtown.
☐West of Newport along A3054; take road north to Newtown. Access along public footpath, which follows the sea wall beyond the quay. OS 196: 420 907.

9 Parkhurst Forest
Forestry Commission. Conifer plantations and fine Oak trees. Forest walk starting at picnic place.
☐North-west of Yarmouth; 0.6 miles/1 km along A3054 towards Yarmouth. OS 196: 480 900.

10 Robin Hill Country and Zoological Park
Situated in 80 acres/32 ha of downland, woodland and meadow; nature trail. The zoo has a variety of small mammals, birds and reptiles.
☐Downend, Arreton (Tel: Arreton 430). Open daily, March–November. 2 miles/3 km east of Newport. OS 196: 535 880.

11 The Roman Villa
Noted for its mosaic pavements. A nature trail, following the River Yar, starts nearby at Alverstone (see Nature Trails).
☐Villa is open daily, April–September. South-west of Brading along road to Alverstone. OS 196: 593 862.

12 Sandown Museum
Unique collection of rocks and fossils of the Isle of Wight.
☐High Street, Sandown (Tel: Sandown 404344). Open daily except Sunday.

13 Tropical Bird Park
Over 170 different species of exotic birds including toucans, macaws and cockatoos.
☐Old Park, St Lawrence, Ventnor (Tel: Ventor 852583). Open daily, May–October; November–April, afternoons only 2 miles/3 km west of Ventnor off A3055. OS 196: 522 760.

Kent

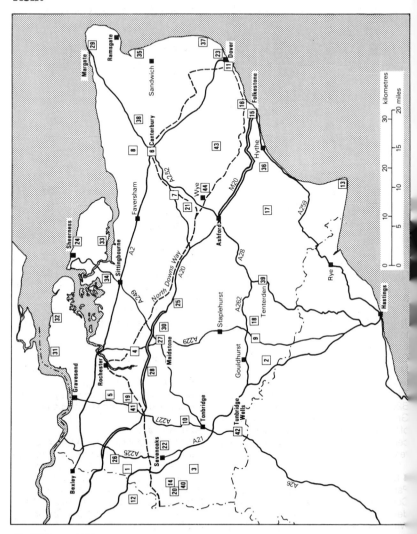

North Downs Way

Long distance route from Farnham to Dover along the Downs of Kent and Surrey. Most of the path runs along the crest of the North Downs and gives fine views of the surrounding countryside; areas of particular interest in Kent are described in the list of places to vist below. The route is well signposted; walkers are advised to keep to paths and to avoid crossing private lan☐The Countryside Commission publish a booklet of maps and a descriptive leaf of the route; available from the Countryside Commission, John Dower Hous Crescent Place, Cheltenham, Glos GL 3RA (Tel: Cheltenham 21381). OS she 178, 179 186, 188, 189.

1 Andrew's Wood, Badger's Mount

Forestry Commission. Variety of trees including Birch, Beech, Larch, Oak, Sweet Chestnut, Ash, Hazel, Hornbeam, and, in places, Sycamore. Broom and Old Man's Beard along outer edges. Bugle, Foxglove, Spotted Orchid, Wild Mint and Yellow Pimpernel grow along rides. Birds present are mainly tits, also Woodpigeon, Turtle Dove and Goldcrest.

☐4½ miles/7 km north of Sevenoaks along A21; take turning east at roundabout with A224. OS 188: 502 616.

2 Bedgebury National Pinetum

Forestry Commission. Over 200 species of conifers. Guide available. Also worth visiting: Bedgebury Forest, which surrounds the pinetum. Woodland birds, butterflies and flowers.

☐4 miles/6.5 km south of Goudhurst (east of Tunbridge Wells along A262) off B2079. OS 188: 720 339.

3 Bough Beech Reservoir

Part of the reservoir is a reserve of the Kent Trust for Nature Conservation. Good place to see birds associated with inland waters, especially in winter; Common Sandpiper, Great Crested and Little Grebes, Heron, Mute Swan, Pintail, Goldeneye, Teal, Tufted Duck, Wigeon, Sparrowhawk.

☐5 miles/8 km west of Tonbridge along B2027. Take road north to Winkhurst Green. Good view from this road just south of Winkhurst Green; Kent Trust Information Centre in old oast house on west side of reservoir. OS 188: 495 485.

4 Burham Down

Part is a reserve of the Kent Trust for Nature Conservation. Chalk downland with some developing scrub. Look out for Weld and Wild Mignonette. Birds include finches and warblers; Jackdaw and Kestrel near quarries.

☐3 miles/5 km north-west of Maidstone, west of A229 along Common Lane (part of the North Downs Way). OS 188: 744 621.

Camer Country Park

Formal park worth visiting for its fine trees; Ash, Beech, Lime, Oak, and Redwood.
☐Open daily. South of Gravesend, near Meopham, on B2009. OS 177: 652 670.

6 Canterbury Royal Museum

Natural history and local history.
☐High Street, Canterbury (Tel: Canterbury 52747). Open daily, except Sunday.

7 Chilham Castle

Castle grounds with lake-side walks, nature trail; pet corner; birds of prey centre.

☐(Tel: Chilham 319 or 654). Grounds open every afternoon, April–October. Enquiries should be made for opening times of birds of prey centre (Tel: Chilham 368). The castle is not open to the public. 6 miles/9.6 km south-west of Canterbury, off A252. OS 179: 069 535.

8 Clowes Wood

Forestry Commission. Varied woodland of different ages. Fine views over Thames estuary when clear. Woodland birds; signposted walk.

☐5 miles/8 km north of Canterbury, on road between Tyler Hill and Chestfield. OS 179: 120 630.

9 Cranbrook Museum

The Boyd Alexander collection of local birds; local history, arts and crafts.
☐Carriers Road, Cranbrook. Open Wednesday and Saturday afternoons only.

10 Dene Park

Forestry Commission. Hardwood and conifer plantations; Japanese Larch, Norway Spruce, Oak, Sweet Chestnut, Western Hemlock. The younger plantations are richer in flowers and shrubs. Finches, Goldcrest, and, in summer, Willow Warbler and Chiffchaff. Forest walk beginning at picnic place.

☐3 miles/4.5 km north-east of Tonbridge along A227; take turning to Claygate. OS 188: 606 511.

11 Dover Museum

Geology exhibits and collection of seashells; local history.
☐Ladywell, Dover (Tel: Dover 201066). Open daily, except Monday and Saturday.

12 Downe House

The home of Charles Darwin. Exhibition of the story of evolution.
☐Luxted Road, Downe (Tel: Orpington 59119). Open afternoons, daily except Monday and Friday; closed in February. OS 177: 432 612.

13 Dungeness

Large area of shingle; birds, migrant butterflies, and flowers. Flowers that can be seen in the area include Bird's Foot Tefoil, Broom, Curled Dock, Evening Primrose, Fennel, Foxglove, Gorse, Lesser Dodder, Mouse-ear Hawkweed, Orache, Restharrow, Sallow, Scentless Mayweed, Sea Beet, Sea Kale, Thrift, Sea Purslane, Stonecrops, Valerian, Viper's Bugloss, Wood Sage, and Yellow Horned Poppy. In spring and summer look out for migrant butterflies such as Large White, Clouded Yellow, Painted Lady and Red Admiral. Migratory birds in spring and summer include Arctic and Black Terns and Bluethroat (mainly autumn). In winter, Divers, Scoters (mainly off-shore) Gannet, Wigeon, Bar-tailed Godwit and other waders can be seen. In summer, Common, Little and Roseate Terns, Ringed Plover, Wheatear, Whinchat, Spotted Flycatcher and warblers occur. Redstart may be seen at the Power Station (open to the public on Wednesday afternoon).
☐Between Hastings and Folkestone, to the south and east of Lydd. Dungeness is the tip of the projection (OS 189: 090 170). Shingle radiates out from this point, covering a large area; to the west of Dungeness are military ranges, so read notices carefully for safe times of access to this area. The following places are of special interest to birdwatchers:
☐**RSPB Reserve.** Reception Centre and bird observatory. Open Wednesday, Thursday, Saturday and Sunday. Signposted off Lydd-Dungeness road.
☐**Gravel pits in Denge Marsh.** These can be seen off the Lydd-Dungeness road.
☐**Sandy shore north of Dungeness**. Waders in winter.
☐**The Patch.** An area of warm water effluent on the seaward side of the power station where birds tend to congregate.

14 Emmetts

National Trust. Woodland and fine garden with rare trees and shrubs.
☐(Tel: Idle Hill 429). Open May–June, Tuesday, Wednesday, Thursday and Sunday: afternoons only; April and July–October, Wednesday and Sunday: afternoons only. Near Idle Hill; 3 miles/5 km south-west of Sevenoaks, off A25 onto unclassified road between Sunridge and Idle Hill. OS 188: 477 524.

15 Folkestone Museum

Giles collection of butterflies and moths; geology and archaeology.
☐Central Library, Grace Hill, Folkestone (Tel: Folkestone 57583). Open daily except Sunday.

16 Folkestone Warren

Chalk cliffs with typical flowers and butterflies.
☐Path to cliffs from Weir Bay Road, on east side of Folkestone. OS 179: 240 373.

17 Ham Street National Nature Reserve

Managed by the Nature Conservancy Council. Fine example of Weald Oakwood with typical plants and butterflies. Leaflet available from the Regional Office at Wye.
☐Access along public footpaths only. About 6 miles/10 km south of Ashford; of B2067 between Hamstreet and Ruckinge. OS 189: 005 335.

18 Hemsted Forest

Forestry Commission. Extensive plantations of different ages; mainly Scots Pine, also foreign evergreens, American Oak, Aspen and Sweet Chestnut. The central part of the forest offers good views across the Weald to the chalk escarpment of the North Downs. Borders of rides support a rich assemblage of flowers. Look out for butterflies on Bramble flowers. Birds present include Chiffchaff (summer) Goldcrest, Jay, Kestrel, Nuthatch, and Sparrowhawk. The Purple Emperor Butterfly may be seen in July.
☐2½ miles/4 km south-west of Cranbrook. Take turning off Sissinghurst to Benenden road, in direction of Goddards Green. OS 188: 812 344.

19 Holly Hill Woods
Woodland on North Downs and view point over Medway gap to Burham Down.
☐2 miles/3.5 km west of Snodland (south of Rochester on A228), beyond Paddlesworth. OS 178: 670 630.

20 Ide Hill
National Trust. Wooded part of the Greensand scarp with views over the Weald. Typical woodland birds.
☐4 miles/6 km south-west of Sevenoaks, on west side of B2042. OS 188: 488 517.

21 Kings Wood, Challock Forest
Forestry Commission. Fine stretch of deciduous and coniferous woodland with Sweet Chestnut coppice. Woodland birds, flowers and butterflies; Roe Deer. Forest walk beginning at car park.
☐Off A251 between Ashford and Faversham. Take minor road eastwards to Wye, just south of crossroads with A252. OS 189: 023 502.

22 Knole House
National Trust. Fine parkland with deer; garden; fifteenth century house.
☐Near Sevenoaks, off A225 (Tel: Sevenoaks 53006). Open April–November, Wednesday–Saturday; afternoons only on Sundays. OS 188: 540 543.

23 Langdon Cliffs
Good locality for typical chalkland flowers; Bulbous Buttercup, Devil's-bit Scabious, Hairy Violet, Harebell, Horseshoe Vetch, Majoram, Thyme, Wild Carrot, etc. Butterflies include Blues, Skippers and Marbled White. Watch out for migrants—Clouded Yellow, Painted Lady and Red Admiral—in summer. Some Hawthorn scrub where birds nest in spring.
☐Just east of Dover. Turn east at top of Castle Hill along unclassified road. OS 179: 340 425.

24 Leas Cliffs, East End
Grassy slopes leading down to the sea; maritime plants and rocks; lumps of iron pyrites can sometimes be picked up on the shore.

☐Take B2008 out of Queenborough-in-Sheppey, turn north to East End, beyond Minster. OS 178: 968 735.

25 Leeds Castle
Interesting castle with pleasant grounds; good collection of waterfowl on the moat.
☐(Tel: Maidstone 65400). Open April–July, September–October, Tuesday, Wednesday, Thursday and Sunday afternoons; afternoons daily in August. OS 188: 835 532.

26 Lullingstone Roman Villa and Lullingstone Park
Remains of Roman villa. River Darenth flows close by, creating a picturesque gap in the North Downs. Lullingstone park has woodland and nature trails; chalkland flowers and typical woodland birds.
☐Villa is open daily, all year. 7 miles/ 11 km north of Sevenoaks, on west side of A225 south of Eynsford. OS 177: 530 650.
☐Park is just south of Eynsford; take road in direction of Wells Hill.

27 Maidstone Museum and Art Gallery
Some natural history exhibits, but check whether these are on display. Also Victoriana, musical instruments, ceramics and paintings.
☐St Faith's Street, Maidstone (Tel: Maidstone 544972). Open daily, all year.

28 Manor Park Country Park
Semi-formal parkland; good variety of birds and trees, including some fine Turkey Oaks. Nature trail leaflet available near car park.
☐Open daily, all year. West Malling, on A228. OS 188: 678 573.

29 Margate Public Aquarium
Large selection of marine, tropical and freshwater fish.
☐Palm Bay Avenue, Palm Bay, Margate (Tel: Thanet 21951). Open daily, all year.

30 Mote Park
Attractive park with fine lake; good for water birds, especially during spring and autumn migration.
☐Eastern edge of Maidstone, off A20.

North Kent Marshes

Extensive marshland lies west and east of
the Medway Estuary and along the Swale
which divides the Isle of Sheppey from the
mainland. Access to the coast is not
always easy, some of the smaller lanes
ending in rough tracks or a farmhouse with
little parking space. Considerable walking
may be involved to reach the coast in some
places. Footpaths are sometimes clearly
marked on concrete slabs, as near High
Halstow, but elsewhere there may be no
signs; it is therefore advisable to consult
Ordnance Survey map 178, on which the
footpaths are marked. The areas lying
inland from the estuarine meadows are
mainly fruit orchards and provide an
interesting approach to the coast. Goldfinch, Barn Owl, Collared Dove, Yellow
Wagtail, Corn Bunting, and Tree Sparrow
are some of the birds which may be seen
here. Prickly Lettuce and Alexanders grow
in the hedgebanks. The marshes and
mudflats themselves are excellent areas
for a wide range of birds.

31 North Kent Marshes: Cliffe Marshes

Extensive water meadows and ditches.
Ducks and waders in winter. Water Rail,
Redshank and Snipe. Patches of scrub
may harbour Nightingale, Reed Bunting,
Yellow Wagtail, and finches. Look out for
Common Tern over water in the old quar-
ries of the area.
□5 miles/8 km north of Rochester along
B2000. Access along footpaths from Cliffe.
OS 178: 720 768; walk southwards towards
old quarries or northwards towards coast-
guards' cottages.

32 North Kent Marshes: Halstow, St Mary's and Allhallows Marshes

Water meadows and extensive mudflats;
good viewing from sea walls. Ducks and
waders; White-fronted Geese in winter.
□These marshes lie north-east of Rochester along the A228. Access to Halstow
Marshes along footpaths from High Halstow, OS 178: 781 754. Access to St Mary's
Marshes along footpaths from St Mary's
Hoo, OS 178: 794 767. Access to Allhallows Marshes along footpath eastwards
from Allhallows, OS 178: 835 777.

33 North Kent Marshes: Isle of Sheppey and Swale Estuary

This area contains some of the best mudflats, water meadows, saltmarshes and
creeks in the South-East. A wide range of
birds are attracted to these areas at all
times, but especially in autumn and winter.
Birds to look out for include waders,
ducks, geese and predators such as
Short-eared Owl, Marsh Harrier and Skua.
This is a large area but numerous footpaths lead to the coast. The Swale Footpath Society publish card packs of walks
in the area and these are available from
local bookshops. The following entries are
a few places that could be visited.
□**Shell Ness.** A National Nature Reserve
managed by the Nature Conservancy
Council. Access only along public footpath, starting at the end of the road that
continues south-east through Leysdown-
on-sea, Isle of Sheppey; walk along sea
wall towards Sayes Court. Information
boards describing habitats. Parking
available at Leysdown. OS 178: 052 682.
□**Elmley Marshes.** A reserve of the RSPB.
Open Wednesday, Saturday and Sunday
only. Keep to footpath. Access from
Kingshill Farm, Isle of Sheppey. OS 178:
939 680.
□**Nagden and Cleve Marshes.** Coastal
area is a reserve of the Kent Trust for
Nature Conservation. Public footpath
along sea wall. Birds on mudflats (winter);
flowers on sea wall and saltmarsh.
Approach from Nagden, 1½ miles/2.5 km
north-east of Faversham. Nagden, OS 178:
032 632. Or approach from road leading
from Seasalter (west of Whitstable) to
Graveney, at point where road turns
inland. OS 179: 062 647.

34 North Kent Marshes: Medway Estuary (south)

Many sea birds including divers in winter.
Excellent for migrant ducks and waders.
□This is a large area lying east of Gilling-
ham. The following places provide access
to the coast:
□North of Upchurch at Ham Green
OS 178: 847 698, a short path leads to the
coast.
□The road from Lower Halstow to Funtor

and beyond runs close by the coast. About 1 mile/1.6 km beyond Funton a footpath leads northwards to the coast and Chetney Marshes. OS 178: 895 687 (beginning of path).

35 Pegwell Bay and Sandwich Bay
Coastal area where RSPB, National Trust and Kent Trust for Nature Conservation have a joint reserve. Good for waders and passage migrants; sand dune flowers and other maritime plants.
☐North-east of Sandwich. The area is privately owned and access is through Sandwich Bay Estate (toll). Nature leaflet is available at toll. Turn north along Princess Drive beside St George's Golf Club. OS 176: 352 578.

36 Port Lympe Zoo Park
Good collection of animals including Wild Boar and Wolf, animals common on the Weald 2000 years ago; some unusual birds such as Emus and Cassowaries. Splendid views across Romney Marsh to the south.
☐Lympe, near Hythe (Tel: Hythe 60618). Open daily. 3 miles/5 km west of Hythe on B2067. OS 179: or 189: 103 352.

37 St Margaret's at Cliffe
Cliff top walk; chalkland flowers.
☐North-east of Dover. Follow B2058 through St Margaret's to coastal lookout. OS 179: 374 452.

38 Stodmarsh
Area of marshland, part of which is a National Nature Reserve managed by the Nature Conservancy Council. Warblers, Bittern, Marsh and Hen Harriers, Water Rail, ducks and swans. Leaflet available at car park, at entrance to reserve. Keep to the Lampen Wall path from Stodmarsh village northwards to Grove Ferry.
☐Stodmarsh village is about 5 miles/8 km north-east of Canterbury off A257. OS 179: 220 605.

39 Tenterden and District Museum
An interesting rural museum with exhibits of crafts, tools, agricultural implements; hop-growing display.

☐Station Road, Tenterden (Tel: Tenterden 2802). Open Easter–October, afternoons daily; mornings also on Saturdays and Sundays. November–Easter, Saturday and Sunday afternoons only.

40 Toys Hill
National Trust. Large area of woodland with some heathland. Typical woodland birds; good views across the Weald.
☐3 miles/5 km south-west of Sevenoaks, off A25 or B2042 onto unclassified road. OS 188: 470 515.

41 Trosley Country Park
On the North Downs Way. Three nature trails; picnic site; typical woodland birds and chalkland flowers on scarp. Information leaflet and nature trail booklet available on site. Information Centre.
☐Open daily, all year. North-east of Sevenoaks, just south of Vigo village. OS 188: 643 612.

42 Tunbridge Wells Museum and Art Gallery
Local natural history, geology and archaeology.
☐Mount Pleasant, Tunbridge Wells (Tel: Tunbridge 26121). Open daily.

43 West Wood, Lyminge Forest
Forestry Commission. Magnificent Douglas Firs, Spruces and other trees; woodland birds. Forest walk beginning at picnic place.
☐9 miles/15 km south of Canterbury along B2068; take unclassified road leading to Elham. OS 179: 138 443.

44 Wye National Nature Reserve
Managed by the Nature Conservancy Council; Information Centre and nature trail. Area of chalk downland with typical flowers and butterflies. Some woodland and fine views southwards to Romney Marsh. Nature trail and Reserve leaflet, available from Information Centre, office in Wye and local bookshops.
☐1½ miles/2 km along road from Wye to Hastingleigh. Information Centre open Sundays in summer only. OS 189: 079 455.

Surrey

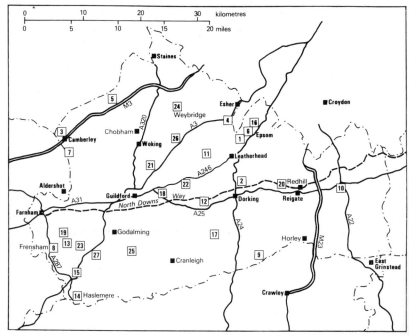

North Downs Way

See entry under Kent for details of this long distance footpath. Areas of particular interest along the Way in Surrey are described in the places to visit listed below.

1 Ashtead Common

Ancient Oakwood; some trees are several hundred years old. Scrub in more open areas. In summer, Blackcap, Garden and Grasshopper Warblers and Whitethroat may be seen. Green Woodpecker, Long-tailed Tit and Nuthatch also present. Butterflies include Green Hairstreak, Dingy Skipper and Silver-washed Fritillary, Brimstone and Small Heath.

☐ 1 mile/1.6 km north of Leatherhead; turn east off A243. OS 187: 167 598.

2 Box Hill

Large National Trust property of woodland and downland including a Country Park and part of the North Downs Way. Fine Beechwoods; mixed Oakwoods grow on

the plateau and Yew trees in Juniper Bottom valley. The steep cliff known as the Whites (on west side of hill above the River Mole) is famous for its Box bushes. Shrubs in various places on the hill provide shelter for finches, warblers (summer) and other small birds. Woodland birds include Kestrel, Nuthatch, Tree Creeper, and Chiffchaff (summer). Chalkland flowers can be found on the scarp and steep sides of dry valleys: look out for Fragrant and Spotted Orchids, and in September, Lady's Tresses Orchid. The property extends north to include White Hill, an area of interest for its birds, insects and woods.

☐ 1 mile/1.5 km north-east of Dorking. OS 187: 180 510. Access off A24 east of Dorking or from unclassified road off B2032 at Pebble Combe (OS 187: 211 528). White Hill can also be approached from the south side of Mickleham Church or from the bridle way off the B2033. Box Hill is a very popular area so avoid weekends if possible. The following places in the vicinity are also of interest:

☐ **Ranmore Common.** National Trust and Forestry Commission. National Trust property has open chalk grassland and woodland, on north side of unclassified road. Forestry Commission land of mixed wood and plantations is good for bird-watching. Access from unclassified road west out of Dorking. National Trust OS 187: 141 503; Forestry Commission OS 187: 127 502.

☐ **Norbury Park.** Interesting wooded chalk slope with fine Beeches and Yews. Path along River Mole has typical riverside flowers; look out also for Kingfishers. Access off A24, 2 miles/3.5 km north of Dorking at level crossing. OS 187: 165 535.

3 Camberley Museum
Good display of British birds.
☐ Knoll Road, Camberley (Tel: Camberley 64483). Open Tuesday–Saturday.

4 Chessington Zoo
One of the major zoos in the South-East. Large collection of mammals and birds.
☐ Leatherhead Road, Chessington (Tel: Epsom 27227). Open daily. 3 miles/5 km north of Leatherhead off A243. OS 187: 174 623.

5 Chobham Common
Mainly open heathland with some boggy areas, which are best avoided. The effect of repeated fires is much in evidence, with areas at different stages of regeneration. Birch and a few Oak trees. Much of the open ground is covered with an alga, *Zygogonium ericetorum*, which is a primary colonizer of sandy soil. Rushes and mosses in the damp valleys. Heathland butterflies and day-flying Emperor Moth. Birds include Nightjar, Stonechat and Linnet (particularly in large patches of Gorse). Look out for the rare Woodlark.
☐ 2 miles/3.2 km north of Chobham at intersection of B383 and B386. OS 176: 970 650.

6 Epsom Common and Stew Ponds
Common with much Bracken and scrub. Good for birds; in summer, the Grasshopper Warbler and rare Red-backed Shrike

occur. Hogweed and Wild Parsnip attract a number of butterflies in summer. The larger pond (artificially created) attracts Little Grebe, Canada Goose and a number of species of duck. Fleabane and Marsh Thistle amongst other plants grow along the pond edges.
☐ The Common lies just west of Epsom; access to ponds from parking place along B280, west of Epsom. OS 187: 183 612.

7 Frimley
Flooded gravel workings where Waders, Ducks, Warblers and Kingfishers may be seen.
☐ Path leads from near Frimley railway station. Frimley lies just south of Camberley. OS 186: 875 577.

8 Frensham Common and Ponds
Old fishponds surrounded by superb heathland. Water birds on ponds. Buzzard, Goldcrest, Redstart, Stonechat, Tree Pipit and warblers on heathland. Typical flowers around ponds and on heath.
☐ Great Pond is off A287 between Hindhead and Farnham, just south of Frensham. Walk over ridge to Little Pond. OS 186: 847 407.

9 Gatwick Garden Aviaries
Collection of parrots, waterfowl and monkeys. Specialists in breeding endangered species.
☐ Russ Hill, Charlwood (Tel: Norwood Hill 862312). Open daily, Easter–September. 3 miles/5 km south-west of Gatwick roundabout (junction of A23 and A217). Take unclassified road to Charlwood and turn south-west to Russ Hill. OS 187: 231 403.

10 Godstone Bay Pond
Surrey Trust for Nature Conservation reserve. Waterfowl, especially in winter. Canada Goose, Common Sandpiper, Gadwall, Great Crested, Little and Red-necked Grebes, Grey Wagtail, Heron, Kingfisher, Reed Bunting, Reed Warbler, Teal, and Tufted Duck.
☐ East of Redhill along A25, at Godstone. View from public footpath which runs south of the pond. OS 187: 355 516.

11 Great Bookham Common

National Trust. Area of mixed woodlands, scrub and a little open grassland, mostly on heavy clay; several ponds. Some woodland is well matured with fine Oaks and a good understorey of Blackthorn, Hawthorn, Buckthorn, Honeysuckle, Bramble and Holly. Many flowers in woods and by ponds, including Wild Hop and Hemlock. Good variety of woodland butterflies and birds; Treecreeper, Hawfinch, Kestrel, Woodpeckers, Woodcock and in summer, Blackcap, Nightingale, Whitethroat and Lesser Whitethroat; Fieldfare and Redwing in winter. Little Grebe, ducks and geese on ponds. Fox and Roe Deer.
□2 miles/3.5 km west of Leatherhead. Access to car park south off A245 at Cobham. OS 187: 125 565.

12 Hackhurst Downs

National Trust and Surrey Trust for Nature Conservation. Chalk downland and woods on the North Downs. Typical flowers and butterflies. Look out for Spotted and Fragrant Orchids on grasslands.
□5 miles/8 km west of Dorking. Access from south by footpath off A25. OS 187: 095 488.

13 Hankley Common

Ministry of Defence property, but normally open to the public. Bog areas in valleys with typical plants including Sundews. Pine trees are good for birds, especially Crossbill in winter. Interesting heathland flowers.
□3 miles/5 km east of Frensham along unclassified road past Frensham Little Pond. OS 186: 880 410.

14 Haslemere Educational Museum

Natural History exhibits including botany and birds; geology of the Weald. Also archaeology and pre-history.
□High Street, Haslemere (Tel: Haslemere 2112). Open Tuesday–Saturday, also Sunday from April–October.

15 Hindhead

Large National Trust property of heathland, common and woodland. Good selection of flowers, birds and butterflies. Nature trails at Gibbet Hill and in the Devil's Punch Bowl, a wooded valley running north towards Farnham. Nature trail leaflets available from café in car park.
□2 miles/3 km north of Haslemere; each side of A3, north and east of Hindhead. OS 186: 891 357.

16 Horton Country Park

200 acres/81 ha of woodland, grassland and farmland; nature trails and ponds.
□1 mile/1.5 km north-west of Epsom. Access off B280; follow signpost to West Park Farm. OS 187: 190 625.

17 Leith Hill

National Trust. Area of fine Pinewoods. Typical acid soil plants including naturalised *Gaultheria*, a North American plant used for pheasant feed and cover. Tower on Leith Hill Summit, the highest point in the South-East, gives fine views of surrounding counties and the English Channel. The woods of Leith Hill Place are also open to the public and are worth visiting.
□About 5 miles/8 km south-west of Dorking. Access on unclasssified road from Dorking. Car park on road from Leith Hill Place to Abinger Common. Summit can be approached from all sides; from car park, walk east up pathway signposted to tower. Tower is open during the summer. OS 187: 141 433.

18 Newlands Corner

Chalk scarp with many typical flowers and butterflies; Hawthorn scrub on north side of road is good for birds. Fine views of Vale of Holmesdale and Western Heights of the Weald. The South Downs are visible on a clear day.
□2 miles/3.5 km east of Guildford. Access off A25, near junction with A247. OS 186: 045 493.

19 Old Kiln Agricultural Museum

Collection of agricultural implements, dairy and forge; arboretum.
□Reeds Road, Tilford, Farnham (Tel: Frensham 2300). Open March–September, Wednesday, Saturday and Sunday afternoons.

20 Reigate and Colley Hills
National Trust. Open downland with typical chalk grassland flowers. The steep chalk scarp is capped with woodland growing on Clay-with-Flints. Good views to the south of Leith Hill, the Weald and the South Downs.
☐1 mile/1.5 km north of Reigate. Access by foot along paths on North Downs Way, west from A217. OS 187: 250 520.

21 Send and Papercourt
Flooded gravel workings. Good for ducks and other water birds.
☐2 miles/3.5 km south-east of Woking along A247; at Send, take unclassified road to Pyrford; good views from road. OS 186: 035 564.

22 Sheepleas
Area of chalk grassland and woodland. Beechwoods on western edge contain Dog's Mercury and, in May and June, White Helleborine. Ash, Hazel, Oak, Whitebeam, and a few Yews also occur, interspersed with Dog Rose, Honeysuckle and Wayfaring Tree. Good variety of chalkland flowers on open grassland. Woodland and downland butterflies. Birds include Great Spotted Woodpecker, Green Woodpecker (look out for their holes in old trees), Tawny Owl and, in summer, Blackcap, Chiffchaff and Wood Warbler. Roe Deer and Foxes in wooded areas.
☐6 miles/10 km east of Guildford; signposted off A246. Two parking places, OS 187: 085 514 and 091 510.

23 Thursley Common National Nature Reserve
Nature reserve owned by the Nature Conservancy Council and managed by the Surrey Trust for Nature Conservation. Large tract of open heathland, Pinewoods and some scrub extending eastwards beyond the reserve. Heathland flowers, insects and birds; summer visitors include Hobby, Curlew and Warblers. Great Grey Shrike in autumn. Please avoid bog areas and observe regulations; keep to footpaths.
☐South-east of Farnham along B3001, turn south at Elstead; park at the Moat Pond. OS 186: 905 415.

24 Weybridge Museum
Mainly local history and archaeology; also a collection of birds.
☐Church Street, Weybridge (Tel: Weybridge 43573). Open Monday–Friday, afternoons only; Saturday, mornings also.

25 Winkworth Aboretum
National Trust. Large, open area with two lakes and a fine collection of rare trees and shrubs.
☐(Tel: Wormely 2516). 3 miles/5 km south-east of Godalming, off B2130. OS 186: 990 412.

26 Wisley Gardens
Royal Horticultural Society. Interesting gardens with fine selection of plants; greenhouses.
☐(Tel: Ripley 2163). Open daily (Sunday 10–2 pm for members only). Off A3, south-west of Cobham. OS 187: 063 582.

27 Witley Common
National Trust. Area of open heath and woodland. Information Centre with exhibits on history of the Common and its wildlife; nature trail leaflets. Woodlands mainly of Scots Pine; also Rowan, English, Sessile and Turkey Oaks, Wild Cherry and Wild Service Tree. Heathers, patches of Gorse and Sallow. In some areas lime from old concrete hut bases has allowed plants, not found on acid soils, to establish themselves. Birds in the area include Green Woodpecker, Linnet, Stonechat and Nightingale (summer). Fox and Roe Deer occur.
☐(Tel Wormley 3207). About 2½ miles/ 4 km south-west of Godalming. Access off A286 (where there is a car park) or A3. OS 186: 935 408.

West Sussex

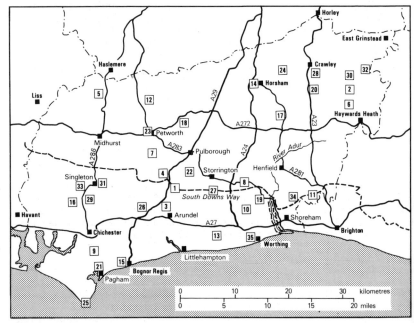

River Adur Footpaths

Public footpaths along both sides of the river for most of the way. Good for water birds and waders, especially in winter.
□ Between Shoreham and Bramber. OS 198: 200 080.

South Downs Way

See entry under East Sussex for details of this long distance path. Areas of particular interest along the Way in West Sussex are described below.

1 Amberley Chalk Pits Museum

History of industries in the South-East; nature and geology trails.
□ (Tel: Bury 370). Open Wednesday–Sunday. 7½ miles/12 km north of Littlehampton; off B2139 between Storrington and the A29.

2 Ardingly Reservoir

A new reservoir where wildlife is beginning to establish itself. Footpaths and bridleways along waters edge and good views from Ardingly to Balcombe road.

□ South-east of Crawley along A23, then B2110 east to Balcombe; footpaths beginning from Balcombe to Ardingly road, OS 187: 318 305 and 332 299.

3 Arundel Park and Wildfowl Trust Refuge

A fine collection of ducks, geese and swans, with hides for close viewing. Situated by Swanbourne Lake in superb downland; good for flowers, birds and butterflies. Information Centre.
□ Mill Road, Arundel (Tel: Arundel 883355). Open daily. 1 mile/1.5 km north of Arundel along unclassified road to Offham. OS 197: 015 090.

4 Bignor Roman Villa and Museum

Interesting mosaic and other remains; picture reconstruction of the Weald as it might have been in Roman times.
□ (Tel: Sutton 259). Open March–October daily except Monday. West of the A29 between Arundel and Pulborough. Access along unclassified road from Bury to Bignor. OS 197: 988 147.

5 Black Down

National Trust. Prominent hill 918 ft/280 m high on sandstone ridge; the highest point in Sussex. Typical heathland vegetation; heath and woodland birds including Meadow Pipit, Yellowhammer, Linnet and Tree Pipit (summer). Nature trail; leaflet available from Black Down Committee, Brownlow House, Portsmouth Road, Hindhead, Surrey.

☐ South-east of Haslemere. Access off B2131 from Haslemere onto unclassified road, then footpath to summit. OS 186: 910 300.

6 Borde Hill Garden

Fine collection of trees and shrubs; good views of countryside; woodland walks.

☐ (Tel: Haywards Heath 50326). Open mid-March–September, Wednesday–Sunday. 1½ miles/2.5 km north of Haywards Heath on road to Balcombe, west of railway. OS 198: 325 265.

7 Burton Park Mill Pond

Good view of lake from the road; look out for unusual birds such as Osprey (winter).

☐ South of Petworth. Access off A285 at Heathland onto unclassified road. OS 197: 980 180.

8 Chanctonbury Ring

Famous landmark of Beech trees and Iron Age camp on South Downs Way. Superb views north across the Weald to Box Hill and Leith Hill, and south to the English Channel.

☐ 6 miles/10 km north of Worthing. Access by footpath only, off A283 at Steyning or off unclassified road at Washington. OS 198: 140 120.

9 Chichester Gravel Pits

Excellent birdwatching area in both summer and winter. Look for waders (in shallow parts), ducks, grebes and Black Tern (summer).

☐ View from unclassified road off B2166 at North Mundham. OS 197: 878 042.

10 Cissbury Ring

National Trust. Site of Neolithic flint mines with remains of Iron Age fort. Scrub and typical chalkland flowers including Spotted and Pyramidal Orchids. Fine views of the South Downs.

☐ 3 miles/5 km north of Worthing. May be reached on unclassified road east out of Findon or by footpath off A24 south of Findon. OS 198: 140 082.

11 Devil's Dyke

Deep valley typical of chalk country; originally formed by a stream which disappeared as the water level in the Chalk dropped. Views from hilltop of Leith Hill, Box Hill and the Isle of Wight. Chalkland flowers down the slopes; finches, warblers and other small birds in the scrub.

☐ On South Downs Way. About 2½ miles/4 km north-west of Brighton. Access off A2038 at Red Hill onto unclassified road. OS 198: 265 110.

12 Ebernoe Common

Sussex Trust for Nature Conservation reserve. Deciduous woodland, mainly Oak and Beech; rich in woodland birds, flowers and insects. Pond; mixed scrub.

☐ 4 miles/7 km north of Petworth along A283; best approached from church about 1 mile/1.5 km along road east of A283. OS 197: 975 278.

13 Highdown Gardens

Garden in and around old chalk quarry with interesting trees and flowers.

☐ (Tel: Worthing 204226). North-west of Worthing, 1 mile/1.5 km north of Ferring; signposted off A259. OS 198: 092 043.

14 Horsham Museum

Natural history exhibits including herbarium and stuffed birds; geology; also dairy and blacksmith's forge.

☐ 9 The Causeway, Horsham (Tel: Horsham 4959). Open Tuesday–Friday, afternoons; all day Saturday.

15 Hotham Park Children's Zoo

General collection of small animals and birds, mainly out-of-doors.

☐ Hotham Park, Bognor Regis (Tel: Bognor Regis 824858). Open daily March–November; December–February, weekends only.

16 Kingley Vale National Nature Reserve

Managed by the Nature Conservancy Council. Information centre and nature trail. Fine old Yew trees, chalkland flowers and magnificent dry valley. Fallow and Roe Deer, Badger and Fox occur on the reserve. Nature trail leaflet available from Information Centre.

☐ Open on Sundays, during most of the year. Access from West Stoke, 3½ miles/ 6 km north-west of Chichester, off B2178. OS 197: 828 087.

17 Leonardslee

Fine collection of Rhododendrons, Azalias and Camellias; several lakes.

☐ (Tel: Lower Beeding 212). Open end of April–June, Wednesday, Thursday and Saturday, Sunday; October, weekends only. Just south of Lower Beeding off A281. OS 198: 211 260.

18 The Mens

Sussex Trust for Nature Conservation reserve. An interesting area of Weald woodland with many different trees and shrubs including Wild Service Tree; rich in woodland flowers, birds, butterflies; also many types of fungi, mosses, liverworts, and ferns. A booklet about the wood is available from Horsham Natural History Society, 33 Churchill Avenue, Horsham (Tel: Horsham 2613).

☐ South-west of Horsham on A272 between Wisborough Green and Petworth; just south of Strood Green. OS 197: 024 237.

19 National Butterfly Museum

Magnificent collection of butterflies and moths from all over the world.

☐ The Street, Bramber (Tel: Steyning 813158). Open daily.

20 Nymans Gardens

National Trust. Woodland and farmland. Fine garden with many interesting and rare flowers and shrubs.

☐ (Tel: Handcross 400321). Open April–October, afternoons daily except Monday and Friday. Near Handcross just off M23/A23. OS 187: 265 294.

21 Pagham Harbour

A local nature reserve; one of the best areas in the South-East for birdwatching, especially in spring and autumn. Extensive tidal mudflats provide food for waders, geese and ducks, and smaller migrants can be seen on the nearby shore; the lagoon south of Pagham Church is another place to watch for birds. In winter look for Bar-tailed and Black-tailed Godwits, Brent Goose, Common Scoter, Red-breasted Merganser, Curlew, Sanderling, Eider Duck, Grey Plover, Dunlin, Turnstone, Redshank and Whimbrel. Migrants include Knot, Little Ringed Plover, Ruff, Greenshank, Curlew Sandpiper and Little Stint. Good selection of saltmarsh plants; Scentless Mayweed, Stinking Groundsel and Yellow Horned Poppy on the shingle. Nature trail starts at Information Centre, signposted on left side of the B2145.

☐ (Tel: Selsey 5200) Information Centre open weekends. 5 miles/8 km south of Chichester. Access off B2145, then by public footpaths around the harbour. Visitors should note that the shingle bar is out of bounds in the nesting season. Information Centre and car park at OS 197: 856 963.

22 Parham Gardens

House with lovely old walled garden.

☐ (Tel: Storrington 2021). Open Easter Sunday–September, Sunday, Wednesday, Thursday; afternoons only. West of Storrington, off A283. OS 197: 060 145.

23 Petworth Park

National Trust. House and park; good herd of Fallow Deer.

☐ (Tel: Petworth 42207). Park open all year; house, April–October, afternoons daily except Monday and Friday. The gardens are not open to the public. In village of Petworth, 5 miles/8 km east of Midhurst. OS 197: 976 218.

24 St Leonards Forest

Forestry Commission. Large area of woodland; ponds and stream in southern part; woodland birds and plants; look out for wild Lily-of-the-Valley.

☐Between Horsham and Crawley. Ponds can be seen from unclassified road that runs from Horsham east to Ashford Cross-ways.

25 Selsey Bill
Fine birdwatching area at most southerly point of West Sussex. Two accessible beaches on west side. East Beach is best in winter and at low tide; good for migrant birds (autumn) especially divers, scoters, skuas, terns.
☐South of Chichester, end of B2145. OS 197: 850 924.

26 Slindon Estate
National Trust. Park with fine Beechwoods; farmland: prehistoric barrows.
☐Park open daily. North of Bognor Regis on A29. OS 197: 960 080.

27 Sullington Hill
Scarp slope on the South Downs (near South Downs Way). Good views from crest northwards over the Weald. Two small chalk quarries on the lower slopes. Scrub and woodland, mainly Ash and Whitebeam. Though the scarp is grazed, chalkland flowers and butterflies can be seen at western end. Corn Bunting, Sky-lark; finches and warblers in scrub area.
☐4 miles/6.5 km north of Worthing along A24 then west on A283; at Storrington, lane leads south to Sullington Hill. OS 198: 092 120.

28 Tilgate Forest Park
Semi-formal park with large area of wood-land and lakes. Look out for ducks especially in winter) and grebes on the lakes. Attractive display of wild roses at east end of large lake. Some fine trees.
☐South of Crawley, on east side of A23. OS 187: 275 346.

29 The Trundle
Iron Age Fort on South Downs. Views north towards Hindhead and south to the Isle of Wight across the coastal plain.
☐5 miles/8 km north-east of Chichester along A286; take road southwards be-tween West Dean and Singleton. OS 197: 876 110.

30 Wakehurst Place
National Trust. Administered by the Royal Botanic Gardens, Kew. Gardens, wood-land, lakes; fine trees and shrubs.
☐(Tel: Ardingly 892701). Open daily. 4 miles/6 km south-east of Crawley. OS 187: 339 314.

31 Weald and Downland Open Air Museum
A 45 acre/18 ha site with historic buil-dings, including a blacksmith's forge and charcoal burner's site. Woodland nature trail; look out for the fine mature Hornbeam trees at the edge of the wood. Popular, so avoid bank holidays if possible.
☐Singleton (Tel: Singleton 348). Open daily August–September; April–August, October–November, daily except Mon-day; December–March, Sunday only. OS 197: 875 128.

32 Weir Wood Reservoir
Many freshwater birds including grebes, ducks and Heron; best during spring and autumn migrations. No access but good viewpoints from road at west end of reser-voir (a bird sanctuary).
☐South of East Grinstead, off B2110 onto unclassified road. OS 187: 380 345.

33 West Dean Park
Interesting arboretum and collection of shrubs.
☐(Tel: Singleton 206). Open April–September, Monday–Friday; afternoons only on Sundays. 5 miles/8 km north of Chichester on A286. OS 197: 865 210.

34 Woods Mill
Headquarters of the Sussex Trust for Nature Conservation. Visitors centre in fascinating old mill; displays; nature trail.
☐Open afternoons daily except Monday and Friday. About 8 miles/13 km north-west of Brighton; 1 mile/1.5 km south of Henfield on A2037. OS 198: 218 138.

35 Worthing Museum and Art Gallery
Small natural history section; local archaeology and crafts.
☐Chapel Road, Worthing (Tel: Worthing 204226). Open daily except Sunday.

Conservation

Britain still offers a variety of habitats rich in wildlife, and areas of wild and beautiful countryside; but these areas are threatened as more land is taken up by industry, housing and agriculture.

When hedgerows are removed and woodlands are cleared, wetlands drained, heaths replaced by forestry plantations, and trees felled indiscriminately, vital habitats are destroyed. The aim of wildlife conservation is to preserve existing habitats and manage them so as to ensure that the species dependent upon these habitats survive.

In Britain the official organization for the conservation of wildlife is the Nature Conservancy Council. They seek to inform farmers, planners and industrialists about environmental problems and to gain their co-operation in caring for the environment. The Council also protects important habitats by setting aside certain areas as nature reserves.

The ultimate responsibility for the survival of our wildlife lies with everyone, if the variety of countryside and wildlife is to remain and be enjoyed by future generations. The Countryside Commission has drawn up guidelines for visitors to the countryside. The main points are listed below.

The Country Code

Guard against all risk of fire.
Fasten all gates.
Keep dogs under proper control.
Keep to the paths across farm land.
Avoid damaging fences, hedges, walls.
Leave no litter.
Safeguard water supplies.
Protect wildlife, wild plants and trees.
Go carefully on country roads.
Respect the life of the countryside.

● *The Conservation of Wild Creatures and Wild Plants Act* makes it illegal to pick certain plants which are so rare as to be endangered, and to uproot *any wild plant* without the landowner's permission.

● *The Bird Protection Act* makes it illegal to take the eggs or disturb any wild bird at its nest.

Conservation in the South-East

The South-East is the most densely populated region in Britain. Numerous towns, busy sea ports, several airports and a network of roads and railways occupy large areas of land. Intensive farming is practised on much of the remaining areas.

Fortunately, chemical pollution of air and water is not normally a serious problem as industry is less extensive in this region than in other parts of the country. The main threat to wildlife in the South-East is disturbance of their habitats by the vast numbers of people who pour into the countryside for weekends and holidays.

Long stretches of the coast have been developed for holidaymakers and now support little wildlife. The limited sand dune areas in particular are now very degraded. The South-East still has extensive saltmarshes and mudflats, which are valuable areas for birdlife, but proposed recreational development at Pagham Harbour in West Sussex and industrial development along the Thames Estuary would seriously encroach upon these habitats.

Inland, the areas of heathland that remain are also under pressure, not so much from development, but from the numbers of people who use these areas for recreation and from the accompanying risk of fire. One species, the Dartford Warbler, has declined in numbers over the past years, partly because of the reduction and destruction of its heathland habitat.

To protect the wildlife of the South-East it is therefore important that any development incorporates provisions for wildlife that may be threatened, and that visitors in the countryside should take particular care not to disturb the wildlife habitats that remain.

Dartford Warbler

Further Reading

The Weald. S. W. Woolridge & F. Goldring (Collins, New Naturalist series: 1960)
The New Forest. C. Tubbs (David & Charles: 1968)
Where to go, What to do in the South. R. & M. Elliot (Heritage Publications: 1980)
The Naturalist in Central Southern England. D. Knowlton (David & Charles: 1973)
The Naturalist in South-East England. S. A. Manning (David & Charles: 1974)
New Forest Guide. (Forestry Commission)
Ashdown Forest. G. Christian (Society of the Friends of Ashdown Forest: 1967)
Wildlife in East Sussex: Some places to see and enjoy natural history. (East Sussex Planning Department: 1980)
The Birds of Kent. J. M. Harrison (Witherby: 1953)
Birds of the North Kent Marshes. E. Gillham & R. Homes (Collins: 1950)

Birds of Hampshire and the Isle of Wight. E. Cohen & J. Taverner (Oxford Illustrated Press: 1972)
Birds in Surrey 1900–1970. D. Parr (Batsford: 1972)
A Guide to the Birds of Sussex. G. des Forges & D. Harber (Oxford University Press: 1963)
Where to Watch Birds. J. Gooders (Deutsch: 1974)
Atlas of the Flora of Kent. E. Philip (Kent Field Club: 1981)
Flora of Hampshire. F. Townsend (Reeve:1904)
The Flora of the Isle of Wight. J. Bevis, R. Kettell & B. Shephard (Isle of Wight Natural History and Archaeological Society: 1978)
Flora of Surrey. J. E. Lousley (David & Charles: 1976)
Sussex Plant Atlas. P. C. Hall (Brighton Museum: 1980)

Useful Addresses

South-East England Tourist Board, Cheviot House, 4–6 Monson Road, Tunbridge Wells, Kent.
Southern Tourist Board, Old Town Hall, Leigh Road, Eastleigh, Hampshire.
RSPB (Royal Society for the Protection of Birds), The Lodge, Sandy, Bedfordshire.
National Trust (Kent & East Sussex Regional Office), Scotney Castle, Lamberhurst, Tunbridge Wells, Kent. (Surrey, West Sussex, Hampshire & the Isle of Wight), Polesden Lacey, Dorking, Surrey.
Forestry Commission, South-East England Conservancy Office, Southampton Road, Lyndhurst, Hampshire.
Nature Conservancy Council (Kent, Surrey & Sussex), Zealds, Church Street, Wye, Ashford, Kent. (Hampshire & Isle of Wight), Shrubbs Hill Road, Lyndhurst, Hampshire.
Countryside Commission, John Dower House, Crescent Place, Cheltenham, Gloucestershire.
Each *County Hall* has an Information Office. Kent: Maidstone; Surrey: Kingston-upon-Thames; East Sussex: Lewes; West Sussex: Chichester; Hampshire: Winchester; Isle of Wight:

Newport.
Kent Trust for Nature Conservation, PO Box 29, Maidstone, Kent.
Kent Ornithological Society, Winnats, Whitehill Road, Meopham, Gravesend, Kent.
Surrey Trust for Nature Conservation, Garden Cottage, Tunbarr, Headley, Epsom, Surrey.
Surrey Bird Club, 51a Palace Road, East Molesey, Surrey.
Juniper Hall Field Centre (The Field Studies Council) , Dorking, Surrey, runs many courses for amateur naturalists.
Sussex Trust for Nature Conservation, Woods Mill, Henfield, Sussex.
Sussex Ornithological Society, Hardanger, Littleworth, Partridge Green, West Sussex.
Hampshire & Isle of Wight Naturalists' Trust, 8 Market Place, Romsey, Hampshire.
Hampshire Ornithological Society, 8 Hood Close, Admiral's Way, Andover, Hampshire.
Isle of Wight Natural History and Archeological Society, 66 Carisbroke Road, Newport, Isle of Wight.

Index

Acknowledgements:
Photographers and Artists

Photographers and paintings are credited by page, from top to bottom, left to right.

Cover: John Jeffrey/NHPA, Heather Angel, Heather Angel, Mark Wilson, Geoffrey Kinns, (painting) Phil Weare/Linden Artists, John Woolverton. *Back cover*: Denise Finney.

Page 1: Patrick Thurston. *Page 3*: Heather Angel. *Pages 4–7 (maps)*: Swanston Associates. *Page 8 (map)*: Swanston Associates. *Page 9*: John Sankey, John Sankey. *Page 10*: A. F. Kersting. *Page 11*: I. C. Rose, John Sankey, Heather Angel, Heather Angel, M. J. Woods, Heather Angel, C. & R. Foord/NHPA, John Mason, John Mason. *Page 12*: Heather Angel, Heather Angel, Heather Angel, John Sankey, John Sankey. *Page 13*: (painting) Denise Finney. *Page 14*: Rod Powley/Aquila, Dennis Green, R. H. Fisher/Aquila. *Page 15*: B. S. Turner, J. F. Young, E. A. Janes/Aquila, K. G. Preston-Mafham/NHPA, John Mason, Heather Angel, John Mason, S. C. Bisserot. *Page 16*: Heather Angel, J F. Young. *Page 17*: Geoffrey Kinns, M. J. Woods, M. K. Lofthouse, I. C. Rose, Robin Fletcher, Heather Angel, I. C. Rose, I. C. Rose. *Page 18*: N. Savonius/NHPA. *Page 19*: John Mason, John Sankey, Heather Angel, M. C. F. Proctor, Martin Withers/Aquila, Dennis Avon & Tony Tilford. *Page 20*: John Mason, (painting) Chris Shields/Wilcock Riley. *Page 21*: A. T. Moffett/Aquila, E. O. Fellowes, M. C. Wilkes/Aquila, S. C. Brown/Aquila, J. F. Young, E. O. Fellowes. *Page 22*: Walter Murray/NHPA. *Page 23*: Heather Angel, J. Good/NHPA, S C. Brown/Aquila, R. H. Bridson, E. Hanumantha Rae/NHPA J. F. Young. *Page 24*: C. & R. Foord, C. & R. Foord/NHPA, Heather Angel. *Page 25*: Robin Fletcher, Heather Angel, Heather Angel, (painting) Alan Harris. *Page 26*: Heather Angel. *Page 27*: John Mason, Heather Angel, B. S. Turner, J. Lawton Roberts/Aquila, J. F. Young. *Page 28*: S. C. Bisserot, Heather Angel, Heather Angel, Heather Angel, Heather Angel, Heather Angel. *Page 29*: A. Wharton/Aquila, Heather Angel, Heather Angel, Heather Angel. *Page 30*: Heather Angel, J. F. Young, Frank Blackburn/NHPA, E. O. Fellowes, F. Blackburn, F. Blackburn/Aquila. *Page 31*: J. F. Young, Heather Angel. *Page 32*: Geoffrey Kinns, J. Breeds, John Mason, John Mason, John Mason. *Page 33*: John Sibbick. *Pages 34–35*: Trevor Boyer. *Page 54*: Chris Shields/Wilcock Riley. *Page 55*: David Wright/Tudor Art, Chris Shields/Wilcock Riley. *Page 56*: Chris Shields/Wilcock Riley. *Pages 57–70*: Hilary Burn. *Page 71*: Hilary Burn, Michelle Emblem/Middletons, Hilary Burn. *Pages 72–78*: Hilary Burn. *Pages 79–80*: Joyce Bee. *Page 81*: Joyce Bee, Chris Shields/Wilcock Riley. *Page 82*: Joyce Bee. *Pages 83–85*: John Barber. *Page 86*: John Barber, Michelle Emblem/Middletons. *Pages 87–88*: John Barber. *Pages 89–95*: Annabel Milne & Peter Stebbing. *Page 96*: Annabel Milne, Peter Stebbing, Bob Bampton/Garden Studio (Hawthorn). *Page 97*: Heather Angel, *Page 122*: Alan Harris.